D1826745

Human resources management
Complete Self-Assessment Guide

The guidance in this Self-Assessment is based on Human resources management best practices and standards in business process architecture, design and quality management. The guidance is also based on the professional judgment of the individual collaborators listed in the Acknowledgments.

Notice of rights

Trademarks

Table of Contents

About The Art of Service

The Art of Service, Business Process Architects since 2000, is dedicated to helping stakeholders achieve excellence.

Defining, designing, creating, and implementing a process to solve a stakeholders challenge or meet an objective is the most valuable role… In EVERY group, company, organization and department.

Unless you're talking a one-time, single-use project, there should be a process. Whether that process is managed and implemented by humans, AI, or a combination of the two, it needs to be designed by someone with a complex enough perspective to ask the right questions.

Someone capable of asking the right questions and step back and say, 'What are we really trying to accomplish here? And is there a different way to look at it?'

With The Art of Service's Standard Requirements Self-Assessments, we empower people who can do just that — whether their title is marketer, entrepreneur, manager, salesperson, consultant, Business Process Manager, executive assistant, IT Manager, CIO etc... —they are the people who rule the future. They are people who watch the process as it happens, and ask the right questions to make the process work better.

Contact us when you need any support with this Self-Assessment and any help with templates, blue-prints and examples of standard documents you might need:

http://theartofservice.com
service@theartofservice.com

Acknowledgments

This checklist was developed under the auspices of The Art of Service, chaired by Gerardus Blokdyk.

Representatives from several client companies participated in the preparation of this Self-Assessment.

In addition, we are thankful for the design and printing services provided.

Included Resources - how to access

Included with your purchase of the book is the Human resources management Self-Assessment Spreadsheet Dashboard which contains all questions and Self-Assessment areas and auto-generates insights, graphs, and project RACI planning - all with examples to get you started right away.

How? Simply send an email to
access@theartofservice.com
with this books' title in the subject to get the Human resources management Self Assessment Tool right away.

You will receive the following contents with New and Updated specific criteria:

• The latest quick edition of the book in PDF

• The latest complete edition of the book in PDF, which criteria correspond to the criteria in...

• The Self-Assessment Excel Dashboard, and...

• Example pre-filled Self-Assessment Excel Dashboard to get familiar with results generation

• In-depth specific Checklists covering the topic

• Project management checklists and templates to assist with implementation

INCLUDES LIFETIME SELF ASSESSMENT UPDATES

Every self assessment comes with Lifetime Updates and Lifetime Free Updated Books. Lifetime Updates is an industry-first feature which allows you to receive verified self assessment updates, ensuring you always have the most accurate information at your fingertips.

Get it now- you will be glad you did - do it now, before you forget.

Send an email to **access@theartofservice.com** with this books' title in the subject to get the Human resources management Self Assessment Tool right away.

Your feedback is invaluable to us

If you recently bought this book, we would love to hear from you! You can do this by writing a review on amazon (or the online store where you purchased this book) about your last purchase! As part of our continual service improvement process, we love to hear real client experiences and feedback.

How does it work?
To post a review on Amazon, just log in to your account and click on the Create Your Own Review button (under Customer Reviews) of the relevant product page. You can find examples of product reviews in Amazon. If you purchased from another online store, simply follow their procedures.

What happens when I submit my review?
Once you have submitted your review, send us an email at review@theartofservice.com with the link to your review so we can properly thank you for your feedback.

Purpose of this Self-Assessment

This Self-Assessment has been developed to improve understanding of the requirements and elements of Human resources management, based on best practices and standards in business process architecture, design and quality management.

It is designed to allow for a rapid Self-Assessment to determine how closely existing management practices and procedures correspond to the elements of the Self-Assessment.

The criteria of requirements and elements of Human resources management have been rephrased in the format of a Self-Assessment questionnaire, with a seven-criterion scoring system, as explained in this document.

In this format, even with limited background knowledge of

Human resources management, a manager can quickly review existing operations to determine how they measure up to the standards. This in turn can serve as the starting point of a 'gap analysis' to identify management tools or system elements that might usefully be implemented in the organization to help improve overall performance.

How to use the Self-Assessment

On the following pages are a series of questions to identify to what extent your Human resources management initiative is complete in comparison to the requirements set in standards.

To facilitate answering the questions, there is a space in front of each question to enter a score on a scale of '1' to '5'.

1 Strongly Disagree

2 Disagree

3 Neutral

4 Agree

5 Strongly Agree

Read the question and rate it with the following in front of mind:

'In my belief, the answer to this question is clearly defined'.

There are two ways in which you can choose to interpret this statement;
1. how aware are you that the answer to the question is clearly defined
2. for more in-depth analysis you can choose to gather

evidence and confirm the answer to the question. This obviously will take more time, most Self-Assessment users opt for the first way to interpret the question and dig deeper later on based on the outcome of the overall Self-Assessment.

A score of '1' would mean that the answer is not clear at all, where a '5' would mean the answer is crystal clear and defined. Leave emtpy when the question is not applicable or you don't want to answer it, you can skip it without affecting your score. Write your score in the space provided.

After you have responded to all the appropriate statements in each section, compute your average score for that section, using the formula provided, and round to the nearest tenth. Then transfer to the corresponding spoke in the Human resources management Scorecard on the second next page of the Self-Assessment.

Your completed Human resources management Scorecard will give you a clear presentation of which Human resources management areas need attention.

Human resources management Scorecard Example

Example of how the finalized Scorecard can look like:

Human resources management Scorecard

Your Scores:

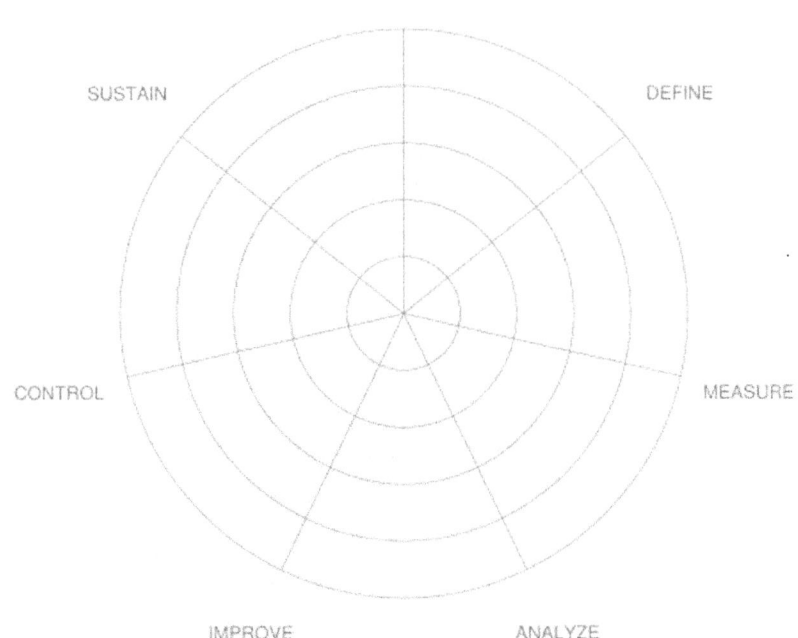

BEGINNING OF THE SELF-ASSESSMENT:

CRITERION #1: RECOGNIZE

INTENT: Be aware of the need for change. Recognize that there is an unfavorable variation, problem or symptom.

In my belief, the answer to this question is clearly defined:

5 Strongly Agree

4 Agree

3 Neutral

2 Disagree

1 Strongly Disagree

1. What do we need to start doing?
<--- Score

2. Will new equipment/products be required to facilitate Human resources management delivery for example is new software needed?
<--- Score

3. What else needs to be measured?

<--- Score

4. Does our organization need more Human resources management education?
<--- Score

5. What should be considered when identifying available resources, constraints, and deadlines?
<--- Score

6. What tools and technologies are needed for a custom Human resources management project?
<--- Score

7. What does Human resources management success mean to the stakeholders?
<--- Score

8. Are there recognized Human resources management problems?
<--- Score

9. What are the stakeholder objectives to be achieved with Human resources management?
<--- Score

10. When a Human resources management manager recognizes a problem, what options are available?
<--- Score

11. Is it clear when you think of the day ahead of you what activities and tasks you need to complete?
<--- Score

12. Are there any specific expectations or concerns about the Human resources management team, Human resources management itself?
<--- Score

13. Are there Human resources management problems defined?
<--- Score

14. How can auditing be a preventative security measure?
<--- Score

15. Will it solve real problems?
<--- Score

16. How do you identify the kinds of information that you will need?
<--- Score

17. What situation(s) led to this Human resources management Self Assessment?
<--- Score

18. How are the Human resources management's objectives aligned to the group's overall stakeholder strategy?
<--- Score

19. Who else hopes to benefit from it?
<--- Score

20. How does it fit into our organizational needs and tasks?
<--- Score

21. How do you assess your Human resources management workforce capability and capacity needs, including skills, competencies, and staffing levels?

<--- Score

22. Will Human resources management deliverables need to be tested and, if so, by whom?

<--- Score

23. Does Human resources management create potential expectations in other areas that need to be recognized and considered?

<--- Score

24. What training and capacity building actions are needed to implement proposed reforms?

<--- Score

25. What vendors make products that address the Human resources management needs?

<--- Score

26. What problems are you facing and how do you consider Human resources management will circumvent those obstacles?

<--- Score

27. Consider your own Human resources management project. what types of organizational problems do you think might be causing or affecting your problem, based on the work done so far?

<--- Score

28. How do we Identify specific Human resources

management investment and emerging trends?
<--- Score

29. What would happen if Human resources management weren't done?
<--- Score

30. Why do we need to keep records?
<--- Score

31. Have you identified your Human resources management key performance indicators?
<--- Score

32. Who defines the rules in relation to any given issue?
<--- Score

33. How do you identify the information basis for later specification of performance or acceptance criteria?
<--- Score

34. What is the smallest subset of the problem we can usefully solve?
<--- Score

35. Think about the people you identified for your Human resources management project and the project responsibilities you would assign to them. what kind of training do you think they would need to perform these responsibilities effectively?
<--- Score

36. Who needs to know about Human resources management ?

<--- Score

37. Are controls defined to recognize and contain problems?
<--- Score

38. How much are sponsors, customers, partners, stakeholders involved in Human resources management? In other words, what are the risks, if Human resources management does not deliver successfully?
<--- Score

39. What are the expected benefits of Human resources management to the stakeholder?
<--- Score

40. How do you prevent errors and rework?
<--- Score

41. What prevents me from making the changes I know will make me a more effective Human resources management leader?
<--- Score

42. What is the smallest subset of the problem we can usefully solve?
<--- Score

43. Will a response program recognize when a crisis occurs and provide some level of response?
<--- Score

44. Do we know what we need to know about this topic?
<--- Score

45. Can Management personnel recognize the monetary benefit of Human resources management?
<--- Score

46. As a sponsor, customer or management, how important is it to meet goals, objectives?
<--- Score

47. How are we going to measure success?
<--- Score

48. For your Human resources management project, identify and describe the business environment. is there more than one layer to the business environment?
<--- Score

49. What information do users need?
<--- Score

Add up total points for this section:
_ _ _ _ _ = Total points for this section

Divided by: _ _ _ _ _ _ (number of statements answered) = _ _ _ _ _ _
Average score for this section

Transfer your score to the Human resources management Index at the beginning of the Self-Assessment.

CRITERION #2: DEFINE:

INTENT: Formulate the stakeholder problem. Define the problem, needs and objectives.

In my belief, the answer to this question is clearly defined:

5 Strongly Agree

4 Agree

3 Neutral

2 Disagree

1 Strongly Disagree

1. In what way can we redefine the criteria of choice in our category in our favor, as Method introduced style and design to cleaning and Virgin America returned glamor to flying?
<--- Score

2. Is the team formed and are team leaders (Coaches and Management Leads) assigned?
<--- Score

3. How can the value of Human resources management be defined?
<--- Score

4. Has everyone on the team, including the team leaders, been properly trained?
<--- Score

5. Are security/privacy roles and responsibilities formally defined?
<--- Score

6. Is the team sponsored by a champion or stakeholder leader?
<--- Score

7. How does the Human resources management manager ensure against scope creep?
<--- Score

8. What would be the goal or target for a Human resources management's improvement team?
<--- Score

9. Will team members perform Human resources management work when assigned and in a timely fashion?
<--- Score

10. Is a fully trained team formed, supported, and committed to work on the Human resources management improvements?
<--- Score

11. Are improvement team members fully trained on

Human resources management?
<--- Score

12. Have all of the relationships been defined properly?
<--- Score

13. Will team members regularly document their Human resources management work?
<--- Score

14. What are the boundaries of the scope? What is in bounds and what is not? What is the start point? What is the stop point?
<--- Score

15. How would you define the culture here?
<--- Score

16. Is the team equipped with available and reliable resources?
<--- Score

17. How would one define Human resources management leadership?
<--- Score

18. Is Human resources management linked to key stakeholder goals and objectives?
<--- Score

19. Are there different segments of customers?
<--- Score

20. Is Human resources management Required?
<--- Score

21. Have specific policy objectives been defined?
<--- Score

22. What constraints exist that might impact the team?
<--- Score

23. Are customers identified and high impact areas defined?
<--- Score

24. Has a high-level 'as is' process map been completed, verified and validated?
<--- Score

25. Is there a completed, verified, and validated high-level 'as is' (not 'should be' or 'could be') stakeholder process map?
<--- Score

26. Has the direction changed at all during the course of Human resources management? If so, when did it change and why?
<--- Score

27. How will the Human resources management team and the group measure complete success of Human resources management?
<--- Score

28. What are the compelling stakeholder reasons for embarking on Human resources management?
<--- Score

29. Are Required Metrics Defined?

<--- Score

30. What are the dynamics of the communication plan?
<--- Score

31. How do senior leaders promote an environment that fosters and requires legal and ethical behavior?
<--- Score

32. Is full participation by members in regularly held team meetings guaranteed?
<--- Score

33. Are different versions of process maps needed to account for the different types of inputs?
<--- Score

34. When are meeting minutes sent out? Who is on the distribution list?
<--- Score

35. Who are the Human resources management improvement team members, including Management Leads and Coaches?
<--- Score

36. What are the rough order estimates on cost savings/opportunities that Human resources management brings?
<--- Score

37. What tools and roadmaps did you use for getting through the Define phase?
<--- Score

38. If substitutes have been appointed, have they been briefed on the Human resources management goals and received regular communications as to the progress to date?
<--- Score

39. Is the improvement team aware of the different versions of a process: what they think it is vs. what it actually is vs. what it should be vs. what it could be?
<--- Score

40. Has a team charter been developed and communicated?
<--- Score

41. Does the team have regular meetings?
<--- Score

42. What are the Roles and Responsibilities for each team member and its leadership? Where is this documented?
<--- Score

43. Is it clearly defined in and to your organization what you do?
<--- Score

44. Is the current 'as is' process being followed? If not, what are the discrepancies?
<--- Score

45. In what way can we redefine the criteria of choice clients have in our category in our favor?
<--- Score

46. Has anyone else (internal or external to the group) attempted to solve this problem or a similar one before? If so, what knowledge can be leveraged from these previous efforts?
<--- Score

47. Have all basic functions of Human resources management been defined?
<--- Score

48. What is the minimum educational requirement for potential new hires?
<--- Score

49. Have the customer needs been translated into specific, measurable requirements? How?
<--- Score

50. Are audit criteria, scope, frequency and methods defined?
<--- Score

51. Is there a Human resources management management charter, including stakeholder case, problem and goal statements, scope, milestones, roles and responsibilities, communication plan?
<--- Score

52. How and when will the baselines be defined?
<--- Score

53. Has the improvement team collected the 'voice of the customer' (obtained feedback – qualitative and quantitative)?
<--- Score

54. How do you keep key subject matter experts in the loop?
<--- Score

55. Do we all define Human resources management in the same way?
<--- Score

56. Is the Human resources management scope manageable?
<--- Score

57. Is the team adequately staffed with the desired cross-functionality? If not, what additional resources are available to the team?
<--- Score

58. What organizational structure is required?
<--- Score

59. How will variation in the actual durations of each activity be dealt with to ensure that the expected Human resources management results are met?
<--- Score

60. Has/have the customer(s) been identified?
<--- Score

61. Is Human resources management currently on schedule according to the plan?
<--- Score

62. Is data collected and displayed to better understand customer(s) critical needs and requirements.
<--- Score

63. Are customer(s) identified and segmented according to their different needs and requirements?
<--- Score

64. Is there regularly 100% attendance at the team meetings? If not, have appointed substitutes attended to preserve cross-functionality and full representation?
<--- Score

65. Has the Human resources management work been fairly and/or equitably divided and delegated among team members who are qualified and capable to perform the work? Has everyone contributed?
<--- Score

66. Do the problem and goal statements meet the SMART criteria (specific, measurable, attainable, relevant, and time-bound)?
<--- Score

67. Is the scope of Human resources management defined?
<--- Score

68. Who defines (or who defined) the rules and roles?
<--- Score

69. Are team charters developed?
<--- Score

70. Is there a critical path to deliver Human resources management results?
<--- Score

71. What specifically is the problem? Where does it occur? When does it occur? What is its extent?
<--- Score

72. Are roles and responsibilities formally defined?
<--- Score

73. What critical content must be communicated – who, what, when, where, and how?
<--- Score

74. Are stakeholder processes mapped?
<--- Score

75. What defines Best in Class?
<--- Score

76. When is the estimated completion date?
<--- Score

77. Has a project plan, Gantt chart, or similar been developed/completed?
<--- Score

78. Are there any constraints known that bear on the ability to perform Human resources management work? How is the team addressing them?
<--- Score

79. What key stakeholder process output measure(s) does Human resources management leverage and how?
<--- Score

80. Are accountability and ownership for Human resources management clearly defined?

<--- Score

81. Are task requirements clearly defined?
<--- Score

82. What customer feedback methods were used to solicit their input?
<--- Score

83. Is there a completed SIPOC representation, describing the Suppliers, Inputs, Process, Outputs, and Customers?
<--- Score

84. When was the Human resources management start date?
<--- Score

85. How is the team tracking and documenting its work?
<--- Score

86. How did the Human resources management manager receive input to the development of a Human resources management improvement plan and the estimated completion dates/times of each activity?
<--- Score

87. What baselines are required to be defined and managed?
<--- Score

88. How often are the team meetings?
<--- Score

89. Are approval levels defined for contracts and supplements to contracts?
<--- Score

90. How was the 'as is' process map developed, reviewed, verified and validated?
<--- Score

Add up total points for this section:
_ _ _ _ _ = Total points for this section

Divided by: _ _ _ _ _ _ (number of statements answered) = _ _ _ _ _ _
Average score for this section

Transfer your score to the Human resources management Index at the beginning of the Self-Assessment.

CRITERION #3: MEASURE:

In my belief, the answer to this
question is clearly defined:

5 Strongly Agree

4 Agree

3 Neutral

2 Disagree

1 Strongly Disagree

1. What methods are feasible and acceptable to estimate the impact of reforms?
<--- Score

2. Where is it measured?
<--- Score

3. What are the agreed upon definitions of the high impact areas, defect(s), unit(s), and opportunities that

will figure into the process capability metrics?
<--- Score

4. How Will We Measure Success?
<--- Score

5. Is data collection planned and executed?
<--- Score

6. Who should receive measurement reports ?
<--- Score

7. Who participated in the data collection for measurements?
<--- Score

8. What key measures identified indicate the performance of the stakeholder process?
<--- Score

9. Is performance measured?
<--- Score

10. What are our key indicators that you will measure, analyze and track?
<--- Score

11. Is long term and short term variability accounted for?
<--- Score

12. Which Stakeholder Characteristics Are Analyzed?
<--- Score

13. How is progress measured?
<--- Score

14. Why Measure?
<--- Score

15. Is there a Performance Baseline?
<--- Score

16. What is the total cost related to deploying Human resources management, including any consulting or professional services?
<--- Score

17. How will effects be measured?
<--- Score

18. Is it possible to estimate the impact of unanticipated complexity such as wrong or failed assumptions, feedback, etc. on proposed reforms?
<--- Score

19. What are the uncertainties surrounding estimates of impact?
<--- Score

20. Is key measure data collection planned and executed, process variation displayed and communicated and performance baselined?
<--- Score

21. What measurements are being captured?
<--- Score

22. What data was collected (past, present, future/ongoing)?
<--- Score

23. What are my customers expectations and measures?
<--- Score

24. Do staff have the necessary skills to collect, analyze, and report data?
<--- Score

25. What evidence is there and what is measured?
<--- Score

26. Have you found any 'ground fruit' or 'low-hanging fruit' for immediate remedies to the gap in performance?
<--- Score

27. What to measure and why?
<--- Score

28. How frequently do we track measures?
<--- Score

29. Does Human resources management analysis show the relationships among important Human resources management factors?
<--- Score

30. How can we measure the performance?
<--- Score

31. Which customers can't participate in our market because they lack skills, wealth, or convenient access to existing solutions?
<--- Score

32. What potential environmental factors impact

the Human resources management effort?

<--- Score

33. Is the solution cost-effective?

<--- Score

34. Does Human resources management analysis isolate the fundamental causes of problems?

<--- Score

35. How will you measure your Human resources management effectiveness?

<--- Score

36. What are the types and number of measures to use?

<--- Score

37. Why should we expend time and effort to implement measurement?

<--- Score

38. What has the team done to assure the stability and accuracy of the measurement process?

<--- Score

39. Have all non-recommended alternatives been analyzed in sufficient detail?

<--- Score

40. Are losses documented, analyzed, and remedial processes developed to prevent future losses?

<--- Score

41. How do we focus on what is right -not who is right?

<--- Score

42. What are the costs of reform?
<--- Score

43. Are there any easy-to-implement alternatives to Human resources management? Sometimes other solutions are available that do not require the cost implications of a full-blown project?
<--- Score

44. How do we do risk analysis of rare, cascading, catastrophic events?
<--- Score

45. Are the units of measure consistent?
<--- Score

46. What particular quality tools did the team find helpful in establishing measurements?
<--- Score

47. What are measures?
<--- Score

48. How large is the gap between current performance and the customer-specified (goal) performance?
<--- Score

49. How is Knowledge Management Measured?
<--- Score

50. Among the Human resources management product and service cost to be estimated, which is considered hardest to estimate?

<--- Score

51. Is Process Variation Displayed/Communicated?
<--- Score

52. Which methods and measures do you use to determine workforce engagement and workforce satisfaction?
<--- Score

53. When is Knowledge Management Measured?
<--- Score

54. Why identify and analyze stakeholders and their interests?
<--- Score

55. How do you measure success?
<--- Score

56. How to measure variability?
<--- Score

57. Does the Human resources management task fit the client's priorities?
<--- Score

58. How is the value delivered by Human resources management being measured?
<--- Score

59. Do we effectively measure and reward individual and team performance?
<--- Score

60. Are we taking our company in the direction of

better and revenue or cheaper and cost?

<--- Score

61. Are process variation components displayed/
communicated using suitable charts, graphs, plots?

<--- Score

62. How to measure lifecycle phases?

<--- Score

**63. How frequently do you track Human resources
management measures?**

<--- Score

64. What is an unallowable cost?

<--- Score

65. Are high impact defects defined and identified in
the stakeholder process?

<--- Score

66. What is measured?

<--- Score

67. What about Human resources management
Analysis of results?

<--- Score

68. Was a data collection plan established?

<--- Score

69. What should be measured?

<--- Score

70. How will success or failure be measured?

<--- Score

71. How do senior leaders create a focus on action to accomplish the organization s objectives and improve performance?
<--- Score

72. Will We Aggregate Measures across Priorities?
<--- Score

73. What will be measured?
<--- Score

74. How can you measure Human resources management in a systematic way?
<--- Score

75. Can We Measure the Return on Analysis?
<--- Score

76. Do we aggressively reward and promote the people who have the biggest impact on creating excellent Human resources management services/ products?
<--- Score

77. Can we do Human resources management without complex (expensive) analysis?
<--- Score

78. How are measurements made?
<--- Score

79. What Relevant Entities could be measured?
<--- Score

80. What charts has the team used to display the

components of variation in the process?
<--- Score

81. Have the types of risks that may impact Human resources management been identified and analyzed?
<--- Score

82. How are you going to measure success?
<--- Score

83. What are the key input variables? What are the key process variables? What are the key output variables?
<--- Score

84. Meeting the challenge: are missed Human resources management opportunities costing us money?
<--- Score

85. What are your key Human resources management organizational performance measures, including key short and longer-term financial measures?
<--- Score

86. Have changes been properly/adequately analyzed for effect?
<--- Score

87. How will your organization measure success?
<--- Score

88. Are the measurements objective?
<--- Score

89. What measurements are possible, practicable and

meaningful?
<--- Score

90. Why do the measurements/indicators matter?
<--- Score

91. Is this an issue for analysis or intuition?
<--- Score

92. Customer Measures: How Do Customers See Us?
<--- Score

93. Are you taking your company in the direction of better and revenue or cheaper and cost?
<--- Score

94. Why do measure/indicators matter?
<--- Score

95. Does Human resources management systematically track and analyze outcomes for accountability and quality improvement?
<--- Score

96. Are there measurements based on task performance?
<--- Score

97. How do you identify and analyze stakeholders and their interests?
<--- Score

98. Which customers cant participate in our Human resources management domain because they lack skills, wealth, or convenient access to existing solutions?

<--- Score

99. Are priorities and opportunities deployed to your suppliers, partners, and collaborators to ensure organizational alignment?
<--- Score

100. Is a solid data collection plan established that includes measurement systems analysis?
<--- Score

101. Are key measures identified and agreed upon?
<--- Score

102. What is the right balance of time and resources between investigation, analysis, and discussion and dissemination?
<--- Score

103. Have the concerns of stakeholders to help identify and define potential barriers been obtained and analyzed?
<--- Score

104. Does the practice systematically track and analyze outcomes related for accountability and quality improvement?
<--- Score

105. How will measures be used to manage and adapt?
<--- Score

106. Is data collected on key measures that were identified?
<--- Score

Add up total points for this section:
_____ = Total points for this section

Divided by: _____ (number of
statements answered) = _____
Average score for this section

Transfer your score to the Human
resources management Index at the
beginning of the Self-Assessment.

CRITERION #4: ANALYZE:

INTENT: Analyze causes, assumptions and hypotheses.

In my belief, the answer to this question is clearly defined:

5 Strongly Agree

4 Agree

3 Neutral

2 Disagree

1 Strongly Disagree

1. What are the disruptive Human resources management technologies that enable our organization to radically change our business processes?
<--- Score

2. What tools were used to generate the list of possible causes?
<--- Score

3. How do mission and objectives affect the Human resources management processes of our organization?

<--- Score

4. How do you measure the Operational performance of your key work systems and processes, including productivity, cycle time, and other appropriate measures of process effectiveness, efficiency, and innovation?

<--- Score

5. What other jobs or tasks affect the performance of the steps in the Human resources management process?

<--- Score

6. How is the way you as the leader think and process information affecting your organizational culture?

<--- Score

7. Identify an operational issue in your organization. for example, could a particular task be done more quickly or more efficiently?

<--- Score

8. A compounding model resolution with available relevant data can often provide insight towards a solution methodology; which Human resources management models, tools and techniques are necessary?

<--- Score

9. Is the suppliers process defined and controlled?

<--- Score

10. What process should we select for improvement?
<--- Score

11. What are the revised rough estimates of the financial savings/opportunity for Human resources management improvements?
<--- Score

12. What quality tools were used to get through the analyze phase?
<--- Score

13. What conclusions were drawn from the team's data collection and analysis? How did the team reach these conclusions?
<--- Score

14. Were Pareto charts (or similar) used to portray the 'heavy hitters' (or key sources of variation)?
<--- Score

15. What did the team gain from developing a sub-process map?
<--- Score

16. How do we promote understanding that opportunity for improvement is not criticism of the status quo, or the people who created the status quo?
<--- Score

17. Can we add value to the current Human resources management decision-making process (largely qualitative) by incorporating uncertainty modeling (more quantitative)?
<--- Score

18. Do your employees have the opportunity to do what they do best everyday?
<--- Score

19. What were the financial benefits resulting from any 'ground fruit or low-hanging fruit' (quick fixes)?
<--- Score

20. Think about some of the processes you undertake within your organization. which do you own?
<--- Score

21. Is the suppliers process defined and controlled?
<--- Score

22. Do you, as a leader, bounce back quickly from setbacks?
<--- Score

23. What are your current levels and trends in key Human resources management measures or indicators of product and process performance that are important to and directly serve your customers?
<--- Score

24. What tools were used to narrow the list of possible causes?
<--- Score

25. What controls do we have in place to protect data?
<--- Score

26. What are the best opportunities for value improvement?
<--- Score

27. Think about the functions involved in your Human resources management project. what processes flow from these functions?
<--- Score

28. Do our leaders quickly bounce back from setbacks?
<--- Score

29. Have the problem and goal statements been updated to reflect the additional knowledge gained from the analyze phase?
<--- Score

30. What successful thing are we doing today that may be blinding us to new growth opportunities?
<--- Score

31. What is the cost of poor quality as supported by the team's analysis?
<--- Score

32. What are your current levels and trends in key measures or indicators of Human resources management product and process performance that are important to and directly serve your customers? how do these results compare with the performance of your competitors and other organizations with similar offerings?
<--- Score

33. How do you use Human resources

management data and information to support organizational decision making and innovation?
<--- Score

34. Have any additional benefits been identified that will result from closing all or most of the gaps?
<--- Score

35. Record-keeping requirements flow from the records needed as inputs, outputs, controls and for transformation of a Human resources management process. ask yourself: are the records needed as inputs to the Human resources management process available?
<--- Score

36. What does the data say about the performance of the stakeholder process?
<--- Score

37. Were there any improvement opportunities identified from the process analysis?
<--- Score

38. What other organizational variables, such as reward systems or communication systems, affect the performance of this Human resources management process?
<--- Score

39. Is Data and process analysis, root cause analysis and quantifying the gap/opportunity in place?
<--- Score

40. Was a detailed process map created to amplify critical steps of the 'as is' stakeholder process?

<--- Score

41. When conducting a business process reengineering study, what should we look for when trying to identify business processes to change?
<--- Score

42. An organizationally feasible system request is one that considers the mission, goals and objectives of the organization. key questions are: is the solution request practical and will it solve a problem or take advantage of an opportunity to achieve company goals?
<--- Score

43. Were any designed experiments used to generate additional insight into the data analysis?
<--- Score

44. Where is the data coming from to measure compliance?
<--- Score

45. How was the detailed process map generated, verified, and validated?
<--- Score

46. Did any value-added analysis or 'lean thinking' take place to identify some of the gaps shown on the 'as is' process map?
<--- Score

47. Are gaps between current performance and the goal performance identified?
<--- Score

48. Did any additional data need to be collected?
<--- Score

49. Was a cause-and-effect diagram used to explore the different types of causes (or sources of variation)?
<--- Score

50. How often will data be collected for measures?
<--- Score

51. What are our Human resources management Processes?
<--- Score

52. How does the organization define, manage, and improve its Human resources management processes?
<--- Score

53. Is the performance gap determined?
<--- Score

54. Is the Human resources management process severely broken such that a re-design is necessary?
<--- Score

55. Is the gap/opportunity displayed and communicated in financial terms?
<--- Score

56. What were the crucial 'moments of truth' on the process map?
<--- Score

Add up total points for this section:

_____ = Total points for this section

Divided by: _____ (number of
statements answered) = _____
Average score for this section

Transfer your score to the Human
resources management Index at the
beginning of the Self-Assessment.

CRITERION #5: IMPROVE:

INTENT: Develop a practical solution. Innovate, establish and test the solution and to measure the results.

In my belief, the answer to this question is clearly defined:

5 Strongly Agree

4 Agree

3 Neutral

2 Disagree

1 Strongly Disagree

1. How to Improve?
<--- Score

2. How will we know that a change is improvement?
<--- Score

3. Do we cover the five essential competencies-Communication, Collaboration,Innovation, Adaptability, and Leadership that improve an

organization's ability to leverage the new Human resources management in a volatile global economy?
<--- Score

4. Is there a small-scale pilot for proposed improvement(s)? What conclusions were drawn from the outcomes of a pilot?
<--- Score

5. For estimation problems, how do you develop an estimation statement?
<--- Score

6. How important is the completion of a recognized college or graduate-level degree program in the hiring decision?
<--- Score

7. If you could go back in time five years, what decision would you make differently? What is your best guess as to what decision you're making today you might regret five years from now?
<--- Score

8. What tools were most useful during the improve phase?
<--- Score

9. Are we Assessing Human resources management and Risk?
<--- Score

10. Are the best solutions selected?
<--- Score

11. What is Human resources management's impact

on utilizing the best solution(s)?
<--- Score

12. How can we improve Human resources management?
<--- Score

13. Who will be responsible for documenting the Human resources management requirements in detail?
<--- Score

14. How will you know when its improved?
<--- Score

15. Is the solution technically practical?
<--- Score

16. What is the team's contingency plan for potential problems occurring in implementation?
<--- Score

17. How can skill-level changes improve Human resources management?
<--- Score

18. What evaluation strategy is needed and what needs to be done to assure its implementation and use?
<--- Score

19. What to do with the results or outcomes of measurements?
<--- Score

20. Who controls the risk?

<--- Score

21. Is there a cost/benefit analysis of optimal solution(s)?
<--- Score

22. At what point will vulnerability assessments be performed once Human resources management is put into production (e.g., ongoing Risk Management after implementation)?
<--- Score

23. What attendant changes will need to be made to ensure that the solution is successful?
<--- Score

24. How does the team improve its work?
<--- Score

25. What were the underlying assumptions on the cost-benefit analysis?
<--- Score

26. How do you improve your likelihood of success ?
<--- Score

27. How do we measure improved Human resources management service perception, and satisfaction?
<--- Score

28. How do we measure risk?
<--- Score

29. What lessons, if any, from a pilot were incorporated into the design of the full-scale solution?

<--- Score

30. Are possible solutions generated and tested?
<--- Score

31. How will the group know that the solution worked?
<--- Score

32. How do we improve productivity?
<--- Score

33. What is the implementation plan?
<--- Score

34. Risk events: what are the things that could go wrong?
<--- Score

35. Can the solution be designed and implemented within an acceptable time period?
<--- Score

36. How does the solution remove the key sources of issues discovered in the analyze phase?
<--- Score

37. Risk factors: what are the characteristics of Human resources management that make it risky?
<--- Score

38. Is the measure understandable to a variety of people?
<--- Score

39. Is Supporting Human resources management

documentation required?
<--- Score

40. What actually has to improve and by how much?
<--- Score

41. What error proofing will be done to address some of the discrepancies observed in the 'as is' process?
<--- Score

42. To what extent does management recognize Human resources management as a tool to increase the results?
<--- Score

43. How do you improve workforce health, safety, and security? What are your performance measures and improvement goals for each of these workforce needs and what are any significant differences in these factors and performance measures or targets for different workplace environments?
<--- Score

44. Was a pilot designed for the proposed solution(s)?
<--- Score

45. How do you measure progress and evaluate training effectiveness?
<--- Score

46. How do we keep improving Human resources management?
<--- Score

47. How do you use other indicators, such as workforce retention, absenteeism, grievances, safety, and productivity, to assess and improve workforce engagement?
<--- Score

48. Is the implementation plan designed?
<--- Score

49. What should a proof of concept or pilot accomplish?
<--- Score

50. Do we get business results?
<--- Score

51. What can we do to improve?
<--- Score

52. Who controls key decisions that will be made?
<--- Score

53. How significant is the improvement in the eyes of the end user?
<--- Score

54. How will you measure the results?
<--- Score

55. Who will be using the results of the measurement activities?
<--- Score

56. Is the optimal solution selected based on testing and analysis?
<--- Score

57. How will the team or the process owner(s) monitor the implementation plan to see that it is working as intended?
<--- Score

58. How Do We Link Measurement and Risk?
<--- Score

59. What is the magnitude of the improvements?
<--- Score

60. How do we go about Comparing Human resources management approaches/solutions?
<--- Score

61. For decision problems, how do you develop a decision statement?
<--- Score

62. Is a solution implementation plan established, including schedule/work breakdown structure, resources, risk management plan, cost/budget, and control plan?
<--- Score

63. Are improved process ('should be') maps modified based on pilot data and analysis?
<--- Score

64. Who will be responsible for making the decisions to include or exclude requested changes once Human resources management is underway?
<--- Score

65. Were any criteria developed to assist the team in

testing and evaluating potential solutions?
<--- Score

66. Why improve in the first place?
<--- Score

67. What needs improvement?
<--- Score

68. What is the risk?
<--- Score

69. What tools were used to tap into the creativity and encourage 'outside the box' thinking?
<--- Score

70. What resources are required for the improvement effort?
<--- Score

71. Are new and improved process ('should be') maps developed?
<--- Score

72. Describe the design of the pilot and what tests were conducted, if any?
<--- Score

73. What improvements have been achieved?
<--- Score

74. What does the 'should be' process map/design look like?
<--- Score

75. How do the Human resources management

**results compare with the performance of your
competitors and other organizations with similar
offerings?**
<--- Score

**76. Is there a high likelihood that any
recommendations will achieve their intended
results?**
<--- Score

77. How did the team generate the list of possible
solutions?
<--- Score

**78. Who are the people involved in developing and
implementing Human resources management?**
<--- Score

79. Does the goal represent a desired result that can
be measured?
<--- Score

80. What are the implications of this decision 10
minutes, 10 months, and 10 years from now?
<--- Score

81. Is a contingency plan established?
<--- Score

82. What tools were used to evaluate the potential
solutions?
<--- Score

83. In the past few months, what is the smallest
change we have made that has had the biggest
positive result? What was it about that small change

that produced the large return?
<--- Score

84. How do we Improve Human resources management service perception, and satisfaction?
<--- Score

85. How will you know that you have improved?
<--- Score

86. Are there any constraints (technical, political, cultural, or otherwise) that would inhibit certain solutions?
<--- Score

87. What do we want to improve?
<--- Score

88. How do we decide how much to remunerate an employee?
<--- Score

89. What communications are necessary to support the implementation of the solution?
<--- Score

90. How can we improve performance?
<--- Score

91. What went well, what should change, what can improve?
<--- Score

92. Is pilot data collected and analyzed?
<--- Score

Add up total points for this section:
_____ = Total points for this section

Divided by: _____ (number of
statements answered) = _____
Average score for this section

Transfer your score to the Human
resources management Index at the
beginning of the Self-Assessment.

CRITERION #6: CONTROL:

1. Whats the best design framework for Human resources management organization now that, in a post industrial-age if the top-down, command and control model is no longer relevant?
<--- Score

2. How might the group capture best practices and lessons learned so as to leverage improvements?
<--- Score

3. Does Human resources management appropriately measure and monitor risk?
<--- Score

4. Is there documentation that will support the successful operation of the improvement?
<--- Score

5. What should we measure to verify efficiency gains?
<--- Score

6. Why is change control necessary?
<--- Score

7. In the case of a Human resources management project, the criteria for the audit derive from implementation objectives. an audit of a Human resources management project involves assessing whether the recommendations outlined for implementation have been met. in other words, can we track that any Human resources management project is implemented as planned, and is it working?
<--- Score

8. Do the Human resources management decisions we make today help people and the planet tomorrow?
<--- Score

9. How will report readings be checked to effectively monitor performance?
<--- Score

10. How do our controls stack up?

<--- Score

11. What are the known security controls?
<--- Score

12. Are new process steps, standards, and documentation ingrained into normal operations?
<--- Score

13. Who will be in control?
<--- Score

14. Are pertinent alerts monitored, analyzed and distributed to appropriate personnel?
<--- Score

15. What are the critical parameters to watch?
<--- Score

16. Against what alternative is success being measured?
<--- Score

17. What other systems, operations, processes, and infrastructures (hiring practices, staffing, training, incentives/rewards, metrics/dashboards/scorecards, etc.) need updates, additions, changes, or deletions in order to facilitate knowledge transfer and improvements?
<--- Score

18. Is there a control plan in place for sustaining improvements (short and long-term)?
<--- Score

19. How can we best use all of our knowledge

repositories to enhance learning and sharing?
<--- Score

20. Is reporting being used or needed?
<--- Score

21. What quality tools were useful in the control phase?
<--- Score

22. Does the response plan contain a definite closed loop continual improvement scheme (e.g., plan-do-check-act)?
<--- Score

23. Have new or revised work instructions resulted?
<--- Score

24. Is there a documented and implemented monitoring plan?
<--- Score

25. Do the decisions we make today help people and the planet tomorrow?
<--- Score

26. What are your results for key measures or indicators of the accomplishment of your Human resources management strategy and action plans, including building and strengthening core competencies?
<--- Score

27. How will new or emerging customer needs/ requirements be checked/communicated to orient the process toward meeting the new specifications

and continually reducing variation?
<--- Score

28. What should the next improvement project be that is related to Human resources management?
<--- Score

29. Has the improved process and its steps been standardized?
<--- Score

30. What is your theory of human motivation, and how does your compensation plan fit with that view?
<--- Score

31. Is new knowledge gained imbedded in the response plan?
<--- Score

32. Does a troubleshooting guide exist or is it needed?
<--- Score

33. Are suggested corrective/restorative actions indicated on the response plan for known causes to problems that might surface?
<--- Score

34. Does the Human resources management performance meet the customer's requirements?
<--- Score

35. Are operating procedures consistent?
<--- Score

36. Who has control over resources?
<--- Score

37. How likely is the current Human resources management plan to come in on schedule or on budget?
<--- Score

38. How do controls support value?
<--- Score

39. Is there a recommended audit plan for routine surveillance inspections of Human resources management's gains?
<--- Score

40. How will the day-to-day responsibilities for monitoring and continual improvement be transferred from the improvement team to the process owner?
<--- Score

41. How will input, process, and output variables be checked to detect for sub-optimal conditions?
<--- Score

42. Are controls in place and consistently applied?
<--- Score

43. What should we measure to verify effectiveness gains?
<--- Score

44. What do we stand for--and what are we against?
<--- Score

45. What is the control/monitoring plan?

<--- Score

46. How will the process owner and team be able to hold the gains?
<--- Score

47. If there currently is no plan, will a plan be developed?
<--- Score

48. What key inputs and outputs are being measured on an ongoing basis?
<--- Score

49. Were the planned controls working?
<--- Score

50. Is there a standardized process?
<--- Score

51. What other areas of the group might benefit from the Human resources management team's improvements, knowledge, and learning?
<--- Score

52. How do you encourage people to take control and responsibility?
<--- Score

53. What is your quality control system?
<--- Score

54. How does your workforce performance management system support high-performance work and workforce engagement; consider workforce compensation, reward, recognition, and

incentive practices; and reinforce a customer and business focus and achievement of your action plans?

<--- Score

55. Do we monitor the Human resources management decisions made and fine tune them as they evolve?

<--- Score

56. Who is the Human resources management process owner?

<--- Score

57. Is a response plan in place for when the input, process, or output measures indicate an 'out-of-control' condition?

<--- Score

58. Will existing staff require re-training, for example, to learn new business processes?

<--- Score

59. Who controls critical resources?

<--- Score

60. How will the process owner verify improvement in present and future sigma levels, process capabilities?

<--- Score

61. Does job training on the documented procedures need to be part of the process team's education and training?

<--- Score

62. How do we enable market innovation while

controlling security and privacy?
<--- Score

63. Will any special training be provided for results interpretation?
<--- Score

64. What are we attempting to measure/monitor?
<--- Score

65. Is there a transfer of ownership and knowledge to process owner and process team tasked with the responsibilities.
<--- Score

66. Where do ideas that reach policy makers and planners as proposals for Human resources management strengthening and reform actually originate?
<--- Score

67. Is there a Human resources management Communication plan covering who needs to get what information when?
<--- Score

68. What are the key elements of your Human resources management performance improvement system, including your evaluation, organizational learning, and innovation processes?
<--- Score

69. Were the planned controls in place?
<--- Score

70. Are documented procedures clear and easy to follow for the operators?
<--- Score

71. Implementation Planning- is a pilot needed to test the changes before a full roll out occurs?
<--- Score

72. Are there documented procedures?
<--- Score

73. Is knowledge gained on process shared and institutionalized?
<--- Score

74. Do you monitor the effectiveness of your Human resources management activities?
<--- Score

75. What is our theory of human motivation, and how does our compensation plan fit with that view?
<--- Score

76. Is a response plan established and deployed?
<--- Score

77. What can you control?
<--- Score

78. What is the recommended frequency of auditing?
<--- Score

Add up total points for this section:
_ _ _ _ _ = Total points for this section

Divided by: _____ (number of
statements answered) = _____
Average score for this section

Transfer your score to the Human
resources management Index at the
beginning of the Self-Assessment.

CRITERION #7: SUSTAIN:

INTENT: Retain the benefits.

In my belief, the answer to this question is clearly defined:

5 Strongly Agree

4 Agree

3 Neutral

2 Disagree

1 Strongly Disagree

1. What is the funding source for this project?
<--- Score

2. Why are Human resources management skills important?
<--- Score

3. What is our competitive advantage?
<--- Score

4. Are we changing as fast as the world around us?

<--- Score

5. If we do not follow, then how to lead?
<--- Score

6. What is the overall business strategy?
<--- Score

7. What are the business goals Human resources management is aiming to achieve?
<--- Score

8. What sources do you use to gather information for a Human resources management study?
<--- Score

9. Whom among your colleagues do you trust, and for what?
<--- Score

10. How do we provide a safe environment -physically and emotionally?
<--- Score

11. Legal and contractual - are we allowed to do this?
<--- Score

12. If we weren't already in this business, would we enter it today? And if not, what are we going to do about it?
<--- Score

13. Who are four people whose careers I've enhanced?
<--- Score

14. What is our question?
<--- Score

15. Who uses our product in ways we never expected?
<--- Score

16. Do you see more potential in people than they do in themselves?
<--- Score

17. What threat is Human resources management addressing?
<--- Score

18. Are we making progress? and are we making progress as Human resources management leaders?
<--- Score

19. What will be the consequences to the stakeholder (financial, reputation etc) if Human resources management does not go ahead or fails to deliver the objectives?
<--- Score

20. How do we foster the skills, knowledge, talents, attributes, and characteristics we want to have?
<--- Score

21. How can you negotiate Human resources management successfully with a stubborn boss, an irate client, or a deceitful coworker?
<--- Score

22. What is the purpose of Human resources

management in relation to the mission?
<--- Score

23. In retrospect, of the projects that we pulled the plug on, what percent do we wish had been allowed to keep going, and what percent do we wish had ended earlier?
<--- Score

24. Do we say no to customers for no reason?
<--- Score

25. What are the gaps in my knowledge and experience?
<--- Score

26. What is it like to work for me?
<--- Score

27. Operational - will it work?
<--- Score

28. What will drive Human resources management change?
<--- Score

29. How do senior leaders set organizational vision and values?
<--- Score

30. Who is responsible for ensuring appropriate resources (time, people and money) are allocated to Human resources management?
<--- Score

31. If you had to rebuild your organization without

any traditional competitive advantages (i.e., no killer a technology, promising research, innovative product/service delivery model, etc.), how would your people have to approach their work and collaborate together in order to create the necessary conditions for success?
<--- Score

32. Schedule -can it be done in the given time?
<--- Score

33. If you were responsible for initiating and implementing major changes in your organization, what steps might you take to ensure acceptance of those changes?
<--- Score

34. How do we Lead with Human resources management in Mind?
<--- Score

35. Do Human resources management rules make a reasonable demand on a users capabilities?
<--- Score

36. Is there any existing Human resources management governance structure?
<--- Score

37. How are we doing compared to our industry?
<--- Score

38. Why should people listen to you?
<--- Score

39. How are conflicts dealt with?

<--- Score

40. Are we making progress (as leaders)?
<--- Score

41. What is the important thing that human resources management should do?
<--- Score

42. How important is Human resources management to the user organizations mission?
<--- Score

43. What is your BATNA (best alternative to a negotiated agreement)?
<--- Score

44. We picked a method, now what?
<--- Score

45. What is our Human resources management Strategy?
<--- Score

46. How Do We Know if We Are Successful?
<--- Score

47. What are specific Human resources management Rules to follow?
<--- Score

48. How can we become the company that would put us out of business?
<--- Score

49. Who will provide the final approval of Human

resources management deliverables?
<--- Score

50. Is there a lack of internal resources to do this work?
<--- Score

51. What do we do when new problems arise?
<--- Score

52. How will we ensure we get what we expected?
<--- Score

53. How do we foster innovation?
<--- Score

54. Why study Human Resources management (hrm)?
<--- Score

55. What counts that we are not counting?
<--- Score

56. Do we have enough freaky customers in our portfolio pushing us to the limit day in and day out?
<--- Score

57. But does it really, really work?
<--- Score

58. What current systems have to be understood and/or changed?
<--- Score

59. Do we have the right people on the bus?
<--- Score

60. Have new benefits been realized?
<--- Score

61. How do we go about Securing Human resources management?
<--- Score

62. Are there any disadvantages to implementing Human resources management? There might be some that are less obvious?
<--- Score

63. Who is responsible for errors?
<--- Score

64. Who will use it?
<--- Score

65. Who is On the Team?
<--- Score

66. Are you satisfied with your current role? If not, what is missing from it?
<--- Score

67. Are the criteria for selecting recommendations stated?
<--- Score

68. What is a good product?
<--- Score

69. Will I get fired?
<--- Score

70. Is a Human resources management Team Work effort in place?

<--- Score

71. Who are our customers?

<--- Score

72. What is the estimated value of the project?

<--- Score

73. Why don't our customers like us?

<--- Score

74. What is the range of capabilities?

<--- Score

75. Are new benefits received and understood?

<--- Score

76. Would you rather sell to knowledgeable and informed customers or to uninformed customers?

<--- Score

77. What am I trying to prove to myself, and how might it be hijacking my life and business success?

<--- Score

78. Will there be any necessary staff changes (redundancies or new hires)?

<--- Score

79. What is the craziest thing we can do?

<--- Score

80. Were lessons learned captured and communicated?

<--- Score

81. Is maximizing Human resources management protection the same as minimizing Human resources management loss?
<--- Score

82. Are we paying enough attention to the partners our company depends on to succeed?
<--- Score

83. Do we underestimate the customer's journey?
<--- Score

84. Do you have a vision statement?
<--- Score

85. How do you govern and fulfill your societal responsibilities?
<--- Score

86. What are our long-range and short-range goals?
<--- Score

87. To whom do you add value?
<--- Score

88. Have totally satisfied customers?
<--- Score

89. What did we miss in the interview for the worst hire we ever made?
<--- Score

90. How do we make it meaningful in connecting

Human resources management with what users do day-to-day?

<--- Score

91. Who else should we help?

<--- Score

92. What are the critical success factors?

<--- Score

93. Are there Human resources management Models?

<--- Score

94. Do we have the right capabilities and capacities?

<--- Score

95. Which functions and people interact with the supplier and or customer?

<--- Score

96. How do senior leaders deploy your organizations vision and values through your leadership system, to the workforce, to key suppliers and partners, and to customers and other stakeholders, as appropriate?

<--- Score

97. Will it be accepted by users?

<--- Score

98. How Do We Create Buy-in?

<--- Score

99. What knowledge, skills and characteristics mark a good Human resources management

project manager?
<--- Score

100. What potential megatrends could make our business model obsolete?
<--- Score

101. Think about the kind of project structure that would be appropriate for your Human resources management project. should it be formal and complex, or can it be less formal and relatively simple?
<--- Score

102. Are we making progress?
<--- Score

103. What does your signature ensure?
<--- Score

104. Who are the key stakeholders?
<--- Score

105. When information truly is ubiquitous, when reach and connectivity are completely global, when computing resources are infinite, and when a whole new set of impossibilities are not only possible, but happening, what will that do to our business?
<--- Score

106. What information is critical to our organization that our executives are ignoring?
<--- Score

107. How will we build a 100-year startup?
<--- Score

108. Which models, tools and techniques are necessary?

<--- Score

109. Is the impact that Human resources management has shown?

<--- Score

110. Which criteria are used to determine which projects are going to be pursued or discarded?

<--- Score

111. What are strategies for increasing support and reducing opposition?

<--- Score

112. What would have to be true for the option on the table to be the best possible choice?

<--- Score

113. What would I recommend my friend do if he were facing this dilemma?

<--- Score

114. Have highly satisfied employees?

<--- Score

115. How do we manage Human resources management Knowledge Management (KM)?

<--- Score

116. How will you know that the Human resources management project has been successful?

<--- Score

117. What is Effective Human resources management?
<--- Score

118. What is Tricky About This?
<--- Score

119. What is our formula for success in Human resources management ?
<--- Score

120. What principles do we value?
<--- Score

121. Where is our petri dish?
<--- Score

122. How can we incorporate support to ensure safe and effective use of Human resources management into the services that we provide?
<--- Score

123. Who is the main stakeholder, with ultimate responsibility for driving Human resources management forward?
<--- Score

124. Who are you going to put out of business, and why?
<--- Score

125. Has the investment re-baselined during the past fiscal year?
<--- Score

126. What role have you played in advising on the creation, management of Human Resources

Management Information System?

<--- Score

127. In what ways are Human resources management vendors and us interacting to ensure safe and effective use?

<--- Score

128. In a project to restructure Human resources management outcomes, which stakeholders would you involve?

<--- Score

129. What are the short and long-term Human resources management goals?

<--- Score

130. Are the assumptions believable and achievable?

<--- Score

131. What kind of crime could a potential new hire have committed that would not only not disqualify him/her from being hired by our organization, but would actually indicate that he/she might be a particularly good fit?

<--- Score

132. How do we maintain Human resources management's Integrity?

<--- Score

133. What management system can we use to leverage the Human resources management experience, ideas, and concerns of the people closest to the work to be done?

<--- Score

134. What are all of our Human resources management domains and what do they do?
<--- Score

135. What have we done to protect our business from competitive encroachment?
<--- Score

136. Instead of going to current contacts for new ideas, what if you reconnected with dormant contacts--the people you used to know? If you were going reactivate a dormant tie, who would it be?
<--- Score

137. What is performance excellence?
<--- Score

138. Is Human resources management dependent on the successful delivery of a current project?
<--- Score

139. Who do we want our customers to become?
<--- Score

140. If we got kicked out and the board brought in a new CEO, what would he do?
<--- Score

141. Do your leaders set clear a direction that is aligned with the vision, mission, and values and is cascaded throughout the organization with measurable goals?
<--- Score

142. Am I failing differently each time?
<--- Score

143. What are we challenging, in the sense that Mac challenged the PC or Dove tackled the Beauty Myth?
<--- Score

144. How do you listen to customers to obtain actionable information?
<--- Score

145. What is the mission of the organization?
<--- Score

146. If no one would ever find out about my accomplishments, how would I lead differently?
<--- Score

147. What happens when a new employee joins the organization?
<--- Score

148. How is business? Why?
<--- Score

149. What business benefits will Human resources management goals deliver if achieved?
<--- Score

150. What one word do we want to own in the minds of our customers, employees, and partners?
<--- Score

151. You may have created your customer policies at a time when you lacked resources, technology wasn't up-to-snuff, or low service levels were

the industry norm. Have those circumstances changed?
<--- Score

152. Who will be responsible for deciding whether Human resources management goes ahead or not after the initial investigations?
<--- Score

153. What happens at this company when people fail?
<--- Score

154. What are the success criteria that will indicate that Human resources management objectives have been met and the benefits delivered?
<--- Score

155. What is something you believe that nearly no one agrees with you on?
<--- Score

156. What are your key business, operational, societal responsibility, and human resource strategic challenges and advantages?
<--- Score

157. Among our stronger employees, how many see themselves at the company in three years? How many would leave for a 10 percent raise from another company?
<--- Score

158. Who will determine interim and final deadlines?
<--- Score

159. What role does communication play in the success or failure of a Human resources management project?
<--- Score

160. In the past year, what have you done (or could you have done) to increase the accurate perception of this company/brand as ethical and honest?
<--- Score

161. What are your organizations work systems?
<--- Score

162. Ask yourself: how would we do this work if we only had one staff member to do it?
<--- Score

163. Are we relevant? Will we be relevant five years from now? Ten?
<--- Score

164. Are assumptions made in Human resources management stated explicitly?
<--- Score

165. How do you determine the key elements that affect Human resources management workforce satisfaction? how are these elements determined for different workforce groups and segments?
<--- Score

166. Do I know what I'm doing? And who do I call if I don't?
<--- Score

167. What are your most important goals for

the strategic Human resources management objectives?

<--- Score

168. Is there any reason to believe the opposite of my current belief?

<--- Score

169. What may be the consequences for the performance of an organization if all stakeholders are not consulted regarding Human resources management?

<--- Score

170. What are internal and external Human resources management relations?

<--- Score

171. How do we keep the momentum going?

<--- Score

172. If I had to leave my organization for a year and the only communication I could have with employees was a single paragraph, what would I write?

<--- Score

173. How much contingency will be available in the budget?

<--- Score

174. How do we ensure that implementations of Human resources management products are done in a way that ensures safety?

<--- Score

175. Can we maintain our growth without

detracting from the factors that have contributed to our success?

<--- Score

176. Who have we, as a company, historically been when we've been at our best?

<--- Score

177. Has implementation been effective in reaching specified objectives?

<--- Score

178. Do you have any supplemental information to add to this checklist?

<--- Score

179. Who, on the executive team or the board, has spoken to a customer recently?

<--- Score

180. How likely is it that a customer would recommend our company to a friend or colleague?

<--- Score

181. What external factors influence our success?

<--- Score

182. What are the rules and assumptions my industry operates under? What if the opposite were true?

<--- Score

183. How would our PR, marketing, and social media change if we did not use outside agencies?

<--- Score

184. If our customer were my grandmother, would I

tell her to buy what we're selling?
<--- Score

185. How will we insure seamless interoperability of Human resources management moving forward?
<--- Score

186. What should we stop doing?
<--- Score

187. What stupid rule would we most like to kill?
<--- Score

188. Think of your Human resources management project. what are the main functions?
<--- Score

189. How long will it take to change?
<--- Score

190. How can we become more high-tech but still be high touch?
<--- Score

191. What are the usability implications of Human resources management actions?
<--- Score

192. What was the last experiment we ran?
<--- Score

193. How will we know if we have been successful?
<--- Score

194. What trophy do we want on our mantle?

<--- Score

195. Which Human resources management goals are the most important?
<--- Score

196. If our company went out of business tomorrow, would anyone who doesn't get a paycheck here care?
<--- Score

197. Who is going to care?
<--- Score

198. Is our strategy driving our strategy? Or is the way in which we allocate resources driving our strategy?
<--- Score

199. Do we think we know, or do we know we know ?
<--- Score

200. Where is your organization on the performance excellence continuum?
<--- Score

201. Do you have an implicit bias for capital investments over people investments?
<--- Score

202. Are we / should we be Revolutionary or evolutionary?
<--- Score

203. How much does Human resources management help?
<--- Score

204. How will we know when our strategy has been successful?
<--- Score

205. Do you keep 50% of your time unscheduled?
<--- Score

206. Which individuals, teams or departments will be involved in Human resources management?
<--- Score

207. Who Uses What?
<--- Score

208. How do we engage the workforce, in addition to satisfying them?
<--- Score

209. How to Secure Human resources management?
<--- Score

210. What is an unauthorized commitment?
<--- Score

211. What happens if you do not have enough funding?
<--- Score

212. If there were zero limitations, what would we do differently?
<--- Score

213. Is the Human resources management organization completing tasks effectively and efficiently?

<--- Score

214. Political -is anyone trying to undermine this project?
<--- Score

215. What are the challenges?
<--- Score

216. Did my employees make progress today?
<--- Score

217. Where can we break convention?
<--- Score

218. Why should we adopt a Human resources management framework?
<--- Score

219. What trouble can we get into?
<--- Score

220. Who do we think the world wants us to be?
<--- Score

221. What is a feasible sequencing of reform initiatives over time?
<--- Score

222. How do I stay inspired?
<--- Score

223. How does Human resources management integrate with other stakeholder initiatives?
<--- Score

224. Whose voice (department, ethnic group, women, older workers, etc) might you have missed hearing from in your company, and how might you amplify this voice to create positive momentum for your business?
<--- Score

225. What are the Essentials of Internal Human resources management Management?
<--- Score

226. What is our mission?
<--- Score

227. How to deal with Human resources management Changes?
<--- Score

228. Marketing budgets are tighter, consumers are more skeptical, and social media has changed forever the way we talk about Human resources management. How do we gain traction?
<--- Score

229. What are the basic business activities and data processing operations that are performed in the human resources management (hrm)/payroll cycle?
<--- Score

230. How do we accomplish our long range Human resources management goals?
<--- Score

231. Who sets the Human resources management standards?

<--- Score

232. Is it economical; do we have the time and money?
<--- Score

233. What are the long-term Human resources management goals?
<--- Score

234. What new services of functionality will be implemented next with Human resources management ?
<--- Score

235. Who will manage the integration of tools?
<--- Score

236. Have benefits been optimized with all key stakeholders?
<--- Score

Add up total points for this section:
_ _ _ _ _ = Total points for this section

Divided by: _ _ _ _ _ _ (number of statements answered) = _ _ _ _ _ _
Average score for this section

Transfer your score to the Human resources management Index at the beginning of the Self-Assessment.

Human resources management and Managing Projects, Criteria for Project Managers:

1.0 Initiating Process Group: Human resources management

1. What were things that you did well, and could improve, and how?

2. Were resources available as planned?

3. At which cmmi level are software processes documented, standardized, and integrated into a standard to-be practiced process for your organization?

4. The Human resources management project you are managing has nine stakeholders. How many channel of communications are there between corresponding stakeholders?

5. Who is funding the Human resources management project?

6. What do you need to do?

7. Does it make any difference if you am successful?

8. Were decisions made in a timely manner?

9. Who is behind the Human resources management project?

10. Just how important is your work to the overall success of the Human resources management project?

11. Are identified risks being monitored properly,

are new risks arising during the Human resources management project or are foreseen risks occurring?

12. Mitigate. what will you do to minimize the impact should the risk event occur?

13. Are the Human resources management project team and stakeholders meeting regularly and using a meeting agenda and taking notes to accurately document what is being covered and what happened in the weekly meetings?

14. What are the required resources?

15. Although the Human resources management project manager does not directly manage procurement and contracting activities, who does manage procurement and contracting activities in your organization then if not the PM?

16. Specific - is the objective clear in terms of what, how, when, and where the situation will be changed?

17. What areas does the group agree are the biggest success on the Human resources management project?

18. Do you know the roles & responsibilities required for this Human resources management project?

19. When will the Human resources management project be done?

20. Based on your Human resources management project communication management plan, what worked well?

1.1 Project Charter: Human resources management

21. What metrics could you look at?

22. Did your Human resources management project ask for this?

23. When do you use a Human resources management project Charter?

24. Why do you manage integration?

25. Human resources management project deliverables: what is the Human resources management project going to produce?

26. Why the improvements?

27. Why do you need to manage scope?

28. Name and describe the elements that deal with providing the detail?

29. Strategic fit: what is the strategic initiative identifier for this Human resources management project?

30. For whom?

31. What are the assumptions?

32. Where does all this information come from?

33. Who is the sponsor?

34. Review the general mission What system will be affected by the improvement efforts?

35. What barriers do you predict to your success?

36. Who manages integration?

37. What is in it for you?

38. Who is the Human resources management project Manager?

39. If finished, on what date did it finish?

40. Environmental stewardship and sustainability considerations: what is the process that will be used to ensure compliance with the environmental stewardship policy?

1.2 Stakeholder Register: Human resources management

41. Who are the stakeholders?

42. What opportunities exist to provide communications?

43. How will reports be created?

44. How much influence do they have on the Human resources management project?

45. Is your organization ready for change?

46. How big is the gap?

47. Who is managing stakeholder engagement?

48. How should employers make voices heard?

49. What is the power of the stakeholder?

50. Who wants to talk about Security?

51. What are the major Human resources management project milestones requiring communications or providing communications opportunities?

52. What & Why?

1.3 Stakeholder Analysis Matrix: Human resources management

53. Alliances: with which other actors is the actor allied, how are they interconnected?

54. Who will obstruct/hinder the Human resources management project if they are not involved?

55. What mechanisms are proposed to monitor and measure Human resources management project performance in terms of social development outcomes?

56. Reputation, presence and reach?

57. Legislative effects?

58. Price, value, quality?

59. How do they affect the Human resources management project and its outcomes?

60. What should thwe organizations stakeholders avoid?

61. How can you fill the need to show progress?

62. Why do you care?

63. Advantages of proposition?

64. Which conditions out of the control of the

management are crucial for the achievement of the outputs?

65. How do customers express needs?

66. Marketing - reach, distribution, awareness?

67. What organizational arrangements are planned to ensure the Human resources management project achieves its social development outcomes?

68. Do the stakeholders goals and expectations support or conflict with the Human resources management project goals?

69. Management cover, succession?

70. Guiding question: what is the issue at stake?

71. Usps (unique selling points)?

72. Are there people who ise voices or interests in the issue may not be heard?

2.0 Planning Process Group: Human resources management

73. On which process should team members spend the most time?

74. If task x starts two days late, what is the effect on the Human resources management project end date?

75. Do the partners have sufficient financial capacity to keep up the benefits produced by the programme?

76. Mitigate. what will you do to minimize the impact should a risk event occur?

77. Why is it important to determine activity sequencing on Human resources management projects?

78. What types of differentiated effects are resulting from the Human resources management project and to what extent?

79. Is the schedule for the set products being met?

80. How does activity resource estimation affect activity duration estimation?

81. Are the necessary foundations in place to ensure the sustainability of the results of the Human resources management project?

82. Is the pace of implementing the products of the

program ensuring the completeness of the results of the Human resources management project?

83. Are there efficient coordination mechanisms to avoid overloading the counterparts, participating stakeholders?

84. How will it affect you?

85. What should you do next?

86. Contingency planning. if a risk event occurs, what will you do?

87. What is the difference between the early schedule and late schedule?

88. How are the principles of aid effectiveness (ownership, alignment, management for development results and mutual responsibility) being applied in the Human resources management project?

89. In what ways can the governance of the Human resources management project be improved so that it has greater likelihood of achieving future sustainability?

90. Human resources management project assessment; why did you do this Human resources management project?

91. To what extent is the program helping to influence your organizations policy framework?

92. What good practices or successful experiences or

transferable examples have been identified?

2.1 Project Management Plan: Human resources management

93. What data/reports/tools/etc. do program managers need?

94. Will you add a schedule and diagram?

95. If the Human resources management project is complex or scope is specialized, do you have appropriate and/or qualified staff available to perform the tasks?

96. What went right?

97. What data/reports/tools/etc. do your PMs need?

98. Is there anything you would now do differently on your Human resources management project based on past experience?

99. Why Change?

100. Do the proposed changes from the Human resources management project include any significant risks to safety?

101. What would you do differently what did not work?

102. Are comparable cost estimates used for comparing, screening and selecting alternative plans, and has a reasonable cost estimate been developed

for the recommended plan?

103. What would you do differently?

104. Are the proposed Human resources management project purposes different than a previously authorized Human resources management project?

105. What happened during the process that you found interesting?

106. What is Human resources management project scope management?

107. Did the planning effort collaborate to develop solutions that integrate expertise, policies, programs, and Human resources management projects across entities?

108. If the Human resources management project management plan is a comprehensive document that guides you in Human resources management project execution and control, then what should it NOT contain?

109. Are cost risk analysis methods applied to develop contingencies for the estimated total Human resources management project costs?

110. Are there any scope changes proposed for a previously authorized Human resources management project?

111. Does the implementation plan have an appropriate division of responsibilities?

112. Are there any windfall benefits that would accrue to the Human resources management project sponsor or other parties?

2.2 Scope Management Plan: Human resources management

113. Are actuals compared against estimates to analyze and correct variances?

114. Does the detailed work plan match the complexity of tasks with the capabilities of personnel?

115. Have all unresolved risks been documented?

116. Is there a formal set of procedures supporting Issues Management?

117. Are schedule deliverables actually delivered?

118. Are calculations and results of analyzes essentially correct?

119. Is the quality assurance team identified?

120. How are you planning to maintain the scope baseline and how will you manage scope changes?

121. Is there a set of procedures defining the scope, procedures, and deliverables defining quality control?

122. Are software metrics formally captured, analyzed and used as a basis for other Human resources management project estimates?

123. Are the budget estimates reasonable?

124. Are cause and effect determined for risks when they occur?

125. Do you have the reasons why the changes to your organizational systems and capabilities are required?

126. Materials available for performing the work?

127. Have the personnel with the necessary skills and competence been identified and has agreement for participation in the Human resources management project been reached with the appropriate management?

128. Are adequate resources provided for the quality assurance function?

129. Personnel with expertise?

130. How difficult will it be to do specific activities on this Human resources management project?

131. Has a resource management plan been created?

132. Can each item be appropriately scheduled?

2.3 Requirements Management Plan: Human resources management

133. Will you document changes to requirements?

134. Should you include sub-activities?

135. Did you avoid subjective, flowery or non-specific statements?

136. Could inaccurate or incomplete requirements in this Human resources management project create a serious risk for the business?

137. Who will approve the requirements (and if multiple approvers, in what order)?

138. Will you use an assessment of the Human resources management project environment as a tool to discover risk to the requirements process?

139. How will unresolved questions be handled once approval has been obtained?

140. When and how will a requirements baseline be established in this Human resources management project?

141. What are you counting on?

142. Who will finally present the work or product(s) for acceptance?

143. Describe the process for rejecting the Human resources management project requirements. Who has the authority to reject Human resources management project requirements?

144. Controlling Human resources management project requirements involves monitoring the status of the Human resources management project requirements and managing changes to the requirements. Who is responsible for monitoring and tracking the Human resources management project requirements?

145. In case of software development; Should you have a test for each code module?

146. How will you communicate scheduled tasks to other team members?

147. Do you have an appropriate arrangement for meetings?

148. Is there formal agreement on who has authority to request a change in requirements?

149. Who will do the reporting and to whom will reports be delivered?

150. Are all the stakeholders ready for the transition into the user community?

151. Who is responsible for quantifying the Human resources management project requirements?

2.4 Requirements Documentation: Human resources management

152. Where do you define what is a customer, what are the attributes of customer?

153. Is your business case still valid?

154. Do technical resources exist?

155. How much does requirements engineering cost?

156. Are there any requirements conflicts?

157. What is effective documentation?

158. Can you check system requirements?

159. What can tools do for us?

160. What is your Elevator Speech?

161. What is the risk associated with cost and schedule?

162. The problem with gathering requirements is right there in the word gathering. What images does it conjure?

163. Does your organization restrict technical alternatives?

164. How much testing do you need to do to prove

that your system is safe?

165. Validity. does the system provide the functions which best support the customers needs?

166. Where do system and software requirements come from, what are sources?

167. Is the requirement properly understood?

168. What are current process problems?

169. Is new technology needed?

170. Can the requirement be changed without a large impact on other requirements?

171. How linear / iterative is your Requirements Gathering process (or will it be)?

2.5 Requirements Traceability Matrix: Human resources management

172. How small is small enough?

173. How do you manage scope?

174. Why do you manage scope?

175. How will it affect the stakeholders personally in their career?

176. Why use a WBS?

177. What are the chronologies, contingencies, consequences, criteria?

178. Will you use a Requirements Traceability Matrix?

179. What is the WBS?

180. What percentage of Human resources management projects are producing traceability matrices between requirements and other work products?

181. Do you have a clear understanding of all subcontracts in place?

182. Is there a requirements traceability process in place?

183. Describe the process for approving requirements

so they can be added to the traceability matrix and Human resources management project work can be performed. Will the Human resources management project requirements become approved in writing?

2.6 Project Scope Statement: Human resources management

184. Were key Human resources management project stakeholders brought into the Human resources management project Plan?

185. Who will you recommend approve the change, and when do you recommend the change reviews occur?

186. Are the input requirements from the team members clearly documented and communicated?

187. If there is an independent oversight contractor, have they signed off on the Human resources management project Plan?

188. What should you drop in order to add something new?

189. Have the reports to be produced, distributed, and filed been defined?

190. What are the possible consequences should a risk come to occur?

191. Will the qa related information be reported regularly as part of the status reporting mechanisms?

192. Have the configuration management functions been assigned?

193. Identify how your team and you will create the Human resources management project scope statement and the work breakdown structure (WBS). Document how you will create the Human resources management project scope statement and WBS, and make sure you answer the following questions: In defining Human resources management project scope and the WBS, will you and your Human resources management project team be using methods defined by your organization, methods defined by the Human resources management project management office (PMO), or other methods?

194. Human resources management project lead, team lead, solution architect?

195. Is the Human resources management project manager qualified and experienced in Human resources management project management?

196. Is the quality function identified and assigned?

197. Will this process be communicated to the customer and Human resources management project team?

198. Which risks does the Human resources management project focus on?

199. Elements that deal with providing the detail?

200. What is the most common tool for helping define the detail?

201. Will you need a statement of work?

202. Will an issue form be in use?

2.7 Assumption and Constraint Log: Human resources management

203. No superfluous information or marketing narrative?

204. Model-building: what data-analytic strategies are useful when building proportional-hazards models?

205. Are there nonconformance issues?

206. If it is out of compliance, should the process be amended or should the Plan be amended?

207. Contradictory information between different documents?

208. Would known impacts serve as impediments?

209. Does the system design reflect the requirements?

210. Are there standards for code development?

211. Does the plan conform to standards?

212. Is the amount of effort justified by the anticipated value of forming a new process?

213. Are there processes in place to ensure that all the terms and code concepts have been documented consistently?

214. Does a documented Human resources

management project organizational policy & plan (i.e. governance model) exist?

215. How are new requirements or changes to requirements identified?

216. Have adequate resources been provided by management to ensure Human resources management project success?

217. Security analysis has access to information that is sanitized?

218. How can you prevent/fix violations?

219. Should factors be unpredictable over time?

220. What worked well?

221. Are there procedures in place to effectively manage interdependencies with other Human resources management projects / systems?

222. Is staff trained on the software technologies that are being used on the Human resources management project?

2.8 Work Breakdown Structure: Human resources management

223. What has to be done?

224. Where does it take place?

225. Is it a change in scope?

226. How big is a work-package?

227. How far down?

228. Can you make it?

229. Why is it useful?

230. When do you stop?

231. Is the work breakdown structure (wbs) defined and is the scope of the Human resources management project clear with assigned deliverable owners?

232. How many levels?

233. What is the probability of completing the Human resources management project in less that xx days?

234. What is the probability that the Human resources management project duration will exceed xx weeks?

235. Why would you develop a Work Breakdown

Structure?

236. When would you develop a Work Breakdown Structure?

237. When does it have to be done?

238. How much detail?

239. Who has to do it?

240. How will you and your Human resources management project team define the Human resources management projects scope and work breakdown structure?

241. Do you need another level?

242. Is it still viable?

2.9 WBS Dictionary: Human resources management

243. Can the contractor substantiate work package and planning package budgets?

244. Does the contractors system identify work accomplishment against the schedule plan?

245. Does the contractor require sufficient detailed planning of control accounts to constrain the application of budget initially allocated for future effort to current effort?

246. Detailed schedules which support control account and work package start and completion dates/events?

247. Identify and isolate causes of favorable and unfavorable cost and schedule variances?

248. Appropriate work authorization documents which subdivide the contractual effort and responsibilities, within functional organizations?

249. What is the goal?

250. Is undistributed budget limited to contract effort which cannot yet be planned to CWBS elements at or below the level specified for reporting to the Government?

251. Are current budgets resulting from changes

to the authorized work and/or internal replanning, reconcilable to original budgets for specified reporting items?

252. Does the contractors system description or procedures require that the performance measurement baseline plus management reserve equal the contract budget base?

253. Are the bases and rates for allocating costs from each indirect pool to commercial work consistent with the already stated used to allocate corresponding costs to Government contracts?

254. Are the contractors estimates of costs at completion reconcilable with cost data reported to us?

255. Is work progressively subdivided into detailed work packages as requirements are defined?

256. Authorization to proceed with all authorized work?

257. Wbs elements contractually specified for reporting of status to you (lowest level only)?

258. Are indirect costs charged to the appropriate indirect pools and incurring organization?

259. Is the work done on a work package level as described in the WBS dictionary?

260. Are the procedures for identifying indirect costs to incurring organizations, indirect cost pools, and allocating the costs from the pools to the contracts

formally documented?

261. Does the contractors system provide for accurate cost accumulation and assignment to control accounts in a manner consistent with the budgets using recognized acceptable costing techniques?

2.10 Schedule Management Plan: Human resources management

262. Are staff skills known and available for each task?

263. Are risk triggers captured?

264. Is a process defined to measure the performance of the schedule management process itself?

265. Is the correct WBS element identified for each task and milestone in the IMS?

266. Is the communication plan being followed?

267. Is there general agreement & acceptance of the current status and progress of the Human resources management project?

268. Does the ims include all contract and/or designated management control milestones?

269. After initial schedule development, will the schedule be reviewed and validated by the Human resources management project team?

270. Are all vendor contracts closed out?

271. Are enough systems & user personnel assigned to the Human resources management project?

272. Have reserves been created to address risks?

273. Are meeting objectives identified for each meeting?

274. Has the budget been baselined?

275. Does the resource management plan include a personnel development plan?

276. Can additional resources be added to subsequent tasks to reduce the durations of the already stated tasks?

277. What does a valid Schedule look like?

278. Is an industry recognized mechanized support tool(s) being used for Human resources management project scheduling & tracking?

279. Have key stakeholders been identified?

2.11 Activity List: Human resources management

280. Is infrastructure setup part of your Human resources management project?

281. How will it be performed?

282. How can the Human resources management project be displayed graphically to better visualize the activities?

283. When do the individual activities need to start and finish?

284. Is there anything planned that does not need to be here?

285. How detailed should a Human resources management project get?

286. The wbs is developed as part of a joint planning session. and how do you know that youhave done this right?

287. What is the total time required to complete the Human resources management project if no delays occur?

288. How do you determine the late start (LS) for each activity?

289. Where will it be performed?

290. What went wrong?

291. When will the work be performed?

292. For other activities, how much delay can be tolerated?

293. How much slack is available in the Human resources management project?

294. Are the required resources available or need to be acquired?

295. What is the LF and LS for each activity?

296. What did not go as well?

2.12 Activity Attributes: Human resources management

297. Activity: what is In the Bag?

298. How many resources do you need to complete the work scope within a limit of X number of days?

299. How else could the items be grouped?

300. Time for overtime?

301. Have constraints been applied to the start and finish milestones for the phases?

302. Activity: what is Missing?

303. Resource is assigned to?

304. Have you identified the Activity Leveling Priority code value on each activity?

305. Has management defined a definite timeframe for the turnaround or Human resources management project window?

306. What is the general pattern here?

307. Does your organization of the data change its meaning?

308. Were there other ways you could have organized the data to achieve similar results?

309. Why?

310. What conclusions/generalizations can you draw from this?

311. How difficult will it be to do specific activities on this Human resources management project?

312. Do you feel very comfortable with your prediction?

313. Resources to accomplish the work?

314. What is your organizations history in doing similar activities?

2.13 Milestone List: Human resources management

315. Effects on core activities, distraction?

316. How will the milestone be verified?

317. Sustainable financial backing?

318. Continuity, supply chain robustness?

319. Which path is the critical path?

320. Timescales, deadlines and pressures?

321. Own known vulnerabilities?

322. Insurmountable weaknesses?

323. It is to be a narrative text providing the crucial aspects of your Human resources management project proposal answering what, who, how, when and where?

324. How late can each activity be finished and started?

325. Calculate how long can activity be delayed?

326. Who will manage the Human resources management project on a day-to-day basis?

327. How will you get the word out to customers?

328. Vital contracts and partners?

329. Level of the Innovation?

330. Identify critical paths (one or more) and which activities are on the critical path?

331. What specific improvements did you make to the Human resources management project proposal since the previous time?

2.14 Network Diagram: Human resources management

332. What job or jobs follow it?

333. What are the Major Administrative Issues?

334. How confident can you be in your milestone dates and the delivery date?

335. Will crashing x weeks return more in benefits than it costs?

336. What is the probability of completing the Human resources management project in less that xx days?

337. Are the required resources available?

338. Where do schedules come from?

339. If the Human resources management project network diagram cannot change and you have extra personnel resources, what is the BEST thing to do?

340. What are the Key Success Factors?

341. What activities must occur simultaneously with this activity?

342. Can you calculate the confidence level?

343. How difficult will it be to do specific activities on this Human resources management project?

344. Are the gantt chart and/or network diagram updated periodically and used to assess the overall Human resources management project timetable?

345. What are the tools?

346. What activities must follow this activity?

347. Are you on time?

348. If x is long, what would be the completion time if you break x into two parallel parts of y weeks and z weeks?

349. What activity must be completed immediately before this activity can start?

350. What is the lowest cost to complete this Human resources management project in xx weeks?

351. What can be done concurrently?

2.15 Activity Resource Requirements: Human resources management

352. Organizational Applicability?

353. Why do you do that?

354. What are constraints that you might find during the Human Resource Planning process?

355. Are there unresolved issues that need to be addressed?

356. How do you handle petty cash?

357. How do you manage time?

358. How many signatures do you require on a check and does this match what is in your policy and procedures?

359. Other support in specific areas?

360. When does monitoring begin?

361. Do you use tools like decomposition and rolling-wave planning to produce the activity list and other outputs?

362. What is the Work Plan Standard?

363. Anything else?

364. Which logical relationship does the PDM use most often?

2.16 Resource Breakdown Structure: Human resources management

365. What can you do to improve productivity?

366. Who is allowed to perform which functions?

367. Who is allowed to see what data about which resources?

368. Is predictive resource analysis being done?

369. Why do you do it?

370. What is each stakeholders desired outcome for the Human resources management project?

371. When do they need the information?

372. What is the primary purpose of the human resource plan?

373. Why is this important?

374. What are the requirements for resource data?

375. Which resources should be in the resource pool?

376. Who needs what information?

377. What is the difference between % Complete and % work?

378. Who will use the system?

379. What defines a successful Human resources management project?

380. What is Human resources management project communication management?

2.17 Activity Duration Estimates: Human resources management

381. Is a Human resources management project charter created once a Human resources management project is formally recognized?

382. What Human resources management project was the first to use modern Human resources management project management?

383. What do corresponding sources say about Human resources management project management?

384. Do procedures exist that identify when and how human resources are introduced and removed from the Human resources management project?

385. Are expert judgment and historical information utilized to estimate activity duration?

386. Does the case present a realistic scenario?

387. Briefly describe some key events in the history of Human resources management project management. What Human resources management project was the first to use modern Human resources management project management?

388. How does poking fun at technical professionals communications skills impact the industry and educational programs?

389. It under budget or over budget?

390. What is earned value?

391. Consider the changes in the job market for information technology workers. How does the job market and current state of the economy affect human resource management?

392. Do checklists exist that list frequently performed activities?

393. How do functionality, system outputs, performance, reliability, and maintainability requirements affect quality planning?

394. Is a contract developed which obligates the seller and the buyer?

395. Which tips for taking the PMP exam do you think would be most helpful for you?

396. Research risk management software. Are many products available?

2.18 Duration Estimating Worksheet: Human resources management

397. What is cost and Human resources management project cost management?

398. Value pocket identification & quantification what are value pockets?

399. How can the Human resources management project be displayed graphically to better visualize the activities?

400. Small or large Human resources management project?

401. Is the Human resources management project responsive to community need?

402. What is next?

403. What info is needed?

404. Can the Human resources management project be constructed as planned?

405. Science = process: remember the scientific method?

406. Is this operation cost effective?

407. What work will be included in the Human resources management project?

408. Why estimate time and cost?

409. Done before proceeding with this activity or what can be done concurrently?

410. Does the Human resources management project provide innovative ways for stakeholders to overcome obstacles or deliver better outcomes?

411. What questions do you have?

412. Will the Human resources management project collaborate with the local community and leverage resources?

413. Do any colleagues have experience with your organization and/or RFPs?

2.19 Project Schedule: Human resources management

414. Why do you think schedule issues often cause the most conflicts on Human resources management projects?

415. Activity charts and bar charts are graphical representations of a Human resources management project schedule ...how do they differ?

416. Are there activities that came from a template or previous Human resources management project that are not applicable on this phase of this Human resources management project?

417. How can you fix it?

418. Human resources management project work estimates Who is managing the work estimate quality of work tasks in the Human resources management project schedule?

419. If you can not fix it, how do you do it differently?

420. Why time management?

421. Is the structure for tracking the Human resources management project schedule well defined and assigned to a specific individual?

422. Are activities connected because logic dictates the order in which others occur?

423. How do you use schedules?

424. Was the Human resources management project schedule reviewed by all stakeholders and formally accepted?

425. How detailed should a Human resources management project get?

426. Verify that the update is accurate. Are all remaining durations correct?

427. How much slack is available in the Human resources management project?

428. How does a Human resources management project get to be a year late ?

429. Eliminate unnecessary activities. Are there activities that came from a template or previous Human resources management project that are not applicable on this phase of this Human resources management project?

430. Did the Human resources management project come in under budget?

431. How can slack be negative?

2.20 Cost Management Plan: Human resources management

432. Has a capability assessment been conducted?

433. Will the forecasts be based on trend analysis and earned value statistics?

434. Are vendor invoices audited for accuracy before payment?

435. Is Human resources management project work proceeding in accordance with the original Human resources management project schedule?

436. Is there a formal process for updating the Human resources management project baseline?

437. What will be the split of responsibilities of progress measurement and controls among the owner, contractor, subcontractors, and vendors?

438. What is the work breakdown structure for the Human resources management project?

439. Have the procedures for identifying budget variances been followed?

440. Contractors scope – how will contractors scope be defined when contracts are let?

441. Estimating responsibilities – how will the responsibilities for cost estimating be allocated?

442. Are risk oriented checklists used during risk identification?

443. Has your organization readiness assessment been conducted?

444. Are the payment terms being followed?

445. Is a stakeholder management plan in place that covers topics?

446. Is there an onboarding process in place?

447. Are meeting minutes captured and sent out after the meeting?

448. Forecasts – how will the time and resources needed to complete the Human resources management project be forecast?

449. Are mitigation strategies identified?

450. Does a documented Human resources management project organizational policy & plan (i.e. governance model) exist?

2.21 Activity Cost Estimates: Human resources management

451. What areas does the group agree are the biggest success on the Human resources management project?

452. Who & what determines the need for contracted services?

453. What are the audit requirements?

454. How do you treat administrative costs in the activity inventory?

455. Are cost subtotals needed?

456. What were things that you did very well and want to do the same again on the next Human resources management project?

457. Eac -estimate at completion, what is the total job expected to cost?

458. Based on your Human resources management project communication management plan, what worked well?

459. What defines a successful Human resources management project?

460. How and when do you enter into Human resources management project Procurement

Management?

461. Why do you manage cost?

462. Vac -variance at completion, how much over/ under budget do you expect to be?

463. What cost data should be used to estimate costs during the 2-year follow-up period?

464. What is the last item a Human resources management project manager must do to finalize Human resources management project close-out?

465. What skill level is required to do the job?

466. What areas were overlooked on this Human resources management project?

467. What happens if you cannot produce the documentation for the single audit?

2.22 Cost Estimating Worksheet: Human resources management

468. What can be included?

469. What happens to any remaining funds not used?

470. Is it feasible to establish a control group arrangement?

471. What costs are to be estimated?

472. Will the Human resources management project collaborate with the local community and leverage resources?

473. What is the estimated labor cost today based upon this information?

474. How will the results be shared and to whom?

475. Is the Human resources management project responsive to community need?

476. Does the Human resources management project provide innovative ways for stakeholders to overcome obstacles or deliver better outcomes?

477. Can a trend be established from historical performance data on the selected measure and are the criteria for using trend analysis or forecasting methods met?

478. Who is best positioned to know and assist in identifying corresponding factors?

479. Identify the timeframe necessary to monitor progress and collect data to determine how the selected measure has changed?

480. What additional Human resources management project(s) could be initiated as a result of this Human resources management project?

481. What will others want?

482. What is the purpose of estimating?

483. Ask: are others positioned to know, are others credible, and will others cooperate?

2.23 Cost Baseline: Human resources management

484. What can go wrong?

485. Is there anything you need from upper management in order to be successful?

486. What would the life cycle costs be?

487. Who will use corresponding metrics ?

488. Have all approved changes to the cost baseline been identified and impact on the Human resources management project documented?

489. If you sold 10x widgets on a day, what would the affect on profits be?

490. What does a good WBS NOT look like?

491. How will cost estimates be used?

492. Has the Human resources management projected annual cost to operate and maintain the product(s) or service(s) been approved and funded?

493. Review your risk triggers -have your risks changed?

494. What is cost and Human resources management project cost management?

495. What is the reality?

496. How accurate do cost estimates need to be?

497. What threats might prevent you from getting there?

498. For what purpose ?

499. Have all approved changes to the schedule baseline been identified and impact on the Human resources management project documented?

500. Does a process exist for establishing a cost baseline to measure Human resources management project performance?

501. Has the Human resources management project (or Human resources management project phase) been evaluated against each objective established in the product description and Integrated Human resources management project Plan?

502. On budget?

503. When should cost estimates be developed?

2.24 Quality Management Plan: Human resources management

504. What are your results for key measures/indicators of accomplishment of organizational strategy?

505. How does your organization establish and maintain customer relationships?

506. Diagrams and tables to account for complex concepts and increase overall readability?

507. How many Human resources management project staff does this specific process affect?

508. Who is responsible for approving the qapp?

509. Are there ways to reduce the time it takes to get something approved?

510. Do you keep back-up copies of any data?

511. How do you decide what information to record?

512. Is there a Quality Management Plan?

513. How is staff trained in procedures?

514. Do trained quality assurance auditors conduct the audits as defined in the Quality Management Plan and scheduled by the Human resources management project manager?

515. How are changes to procedures made?

516. How are deviations from procedures handled?

517. Has a Human resources management project Communications Plan been developed?

518. How does your organization ensure the reliability, accuracy, timeliness, security and accessibility of data and information?

519. Account for the procedures used to verify the data quality of the data being reviewed?

520. Documented results available?

2.25 Quality Metrics: Human resources management

521. Are there any open risk issues?

522. Are quality metrics defined?

523. Is quality culture a competitive advantage?

524. What forces exist that would cause them to change?

525. Were number of defects identified?

526. Can you correlate your quality metrics to profitability?

527. If the defect rate during testing is substantially higher than that of the previous release (or a similar product), then ask: Did you plan for and actually improve testing effectiveness?

528. Are documents on hand to provide explanations of privacy and confidentiality?

529. Was the overall quality better or worse than previous products?

530. Has risk analysis been adequately reviewed?

531. What documentation is required?

532. Should a modifier be included?

533. Do you know how much profit a 10% decrease in waste would generate?

534. How does one achieve stability?

535. Which are the right metrics to use?

536. What approved evidence based screening tools can be used?

537. There are many reasons to shore up quality-related metrics, and what metrics are important?

538. Does risk analysis documentation meet standards?

539. What if the biggest risk to your business were the already stated people who do not complain?

540. Have risk areas been identified?

2.26 Process Improvement Plan: Human resources management

541. Modeling current processes is great, and will you ever see a return on that investment?

542. What personnel are the coaches for your initiative?

543. Who should prepare the process improvement action plan?

544. Why quality management?

545. Where are you now?

546. Have the frequency of collection and the points in the process where measurements will be made been determined?

547. What personnel are the change agents for your initiative?

548. Purpose of goal: the motive is determined by asking, why do you want to achieve this goal?

549. Have storage and access mechanisms and procedures been determined?

550. What is the test-cycle concept?

551. Are you meeting the quality standards?

552. Where do you focus?

553. Are you making progress on the goals?

554. Has the time line required to move measurement results from the points of collection to databases or users been established?

555. Are you following the quality standards?

556. What lessons have you learned so far?

557. Where do you want to be?

558. Management commitment at all levels?

559. Have the supporting tools been developed or acquired?

560. Why do you want to achieve the goal?

2.27 Responsibility Assignment Matrix: Human resources management

561. What are the constraints?

562. What expertise is not available in your department?

563. How do you assist them to be as productive as possible?

564. Does the accounting system provide a basis for auditing records of direct costs chargeable to the contract?

565. Which Human resources management project management knowledge area is least mature?

566. Is the anticipated (firm and potential) business base Human resources management projected in a rational, consistent manner?

567. Are there any drawbacks to using a responsibility assignment matrix?

568. Are detailed work packages planned as far in advance as practicable?

569. Does the scheduling system identify in a timely manner the status of work?

570. What expertise is available in your department?

571. Who is going to do that work?

572. Human resources management projected economic escalation?

573. How do you manage remotely to staff in other Divisions?

574. What do you need to implement earned value management?

575. Is work properly classified as measured effort, LOE, or apportioned effort and appropriately separated?

576. Identify potential or actual overruns and underruns?

2.28 Roles and Responsibilities: Human resources management

577. Once the responsibilities are defined for the Human resources management project, have the deliverables, roles and responsibilities been clearly communicated to every participant?

578. What should you do now to prepare yourself for a promotion, increased responsibilities or a different job?

579. Concern: where are you limited or have no authority, where you can not influence?

580. To decide whether to use a quality measurement, ask how will you know when it is achieved?

581. What expectations were NOT met?

582. Are governance roles and responsibilities documented?

583. Who is responsible for implementation activities and where will the functions, roles and responsibilities be defined?

584. Key conclusions and recommendations: Are conclusions and recommendations relevant and acceptable?

585. Have you ever been a part of this team?

586. Authority: what areas/Human resources management projects in your work do you have the authority to decide upon and act on the already stated decisions?

587. Is there a training program in place for stakeholders covering expectations, roles and responsibilities and any addition knowledge others need to be good stakeholders?

588. What should you do now to ensure that you are exceeding expectations and excelling in your current position?

589. Does your vision/mission support a culture of quality data?

590. What is working well?

591. Are your budgets supportive of a culture of quality data?

592. Are Human resources management project team roles and responsibilities identified and documented?

593. Once the responsibilities are defined for the Human resources management project, have the deliverables, roles and responsibilities been clearly communicated to every participant?

594. Required skills, knowledge, experience?

595. What areas would you highlight for changes or improvements?

596. Who is responsible for each task?

2.29 Human Resource Management Plan: Human resources management

597. Does a documented Human resources management project organizational policy & plan (i.e. governance model) exist?

598. Timeline and milestones?

599. Are multiple estimation methods being employed?

600. How do you determine what key skills and talents are needed to meet the objectives. Is your organization primarily focused on a specific industry?

601. Have all necessary approvals been obtained?

602. Is there a formal process for updating the Human resources management project baseline?

603. Are Human resources management project contact logs kept up to date?

604. Are the right people being attracted and retained to meet the future challenges?

605. Are the people assigned to the Human resources management project sufficiently qualified?

606. Are post milestone Human resources management project reviews (PMPR) conducted with your organization at least once a year?

607. Has a Human resources management project Communications Plan been developed?

608. Are change requests logged and managed?

609. Quality assurance overheads?

610. What commitments have been made?

611. List roles. what commitments have been made?

612. Has a quality assurance plan been developed for the Human resources management project?

613. List the assumptions made to date. What did you have to assume to be true to complete the charter?

614. Have Human resources management project management standards and procedures been identified / established and documented?

2.30 Communications Management Plan: Human resources management

615. In your work, how much time is spent on stakeholder identification?

616. Which stakeholders can influence others?

617. Are the stakeholders getting the information others need, are others consulted, are concerns addressed?

618. What to know?

619. What are the interrelationships?

620. Where do team members get information?

621. Who to learn from?

622. What steps can you take for a positive relationship?

623. Can you think of other people who might have concerns or interests?

624. What is Human resources management project communications management?

625. Is the stakeholder role recognized by your organization?

626. Why do you manage communications?

627. Timing: when do the effects of the communication take place?

628. Who is involved as you identify stakeholders?

629. Are there potential barriers between the team and the stakeholder?

630. Are there common objectives between the team and the stakeholder?

631. Who are the members of the governing body?

632. How much time does it take to do it?

633. How is this initiative related to other portfolios, programs, or Human resources management projects?

634. Do you feel more overwhelmed by stakeholders?

2.31 Risk Management Plan: Human resources management

635. How is risk identification performed?

636. What things are likely to change?

637. Litigation – what is the probability that lawsuits will cause problems or delays in the Human resources management project?

638. Is there additional information that would make you more confident about your analysis?

639. Are the required plans included, such as nonstructural flood risk management plans?

640. Are certain activities taking a long time to complete?

641. Do the requirements require the creation of components that are unlike anything your organization has previously built?

642. Has something like this been done before?

643. Where do risks appear in the business phases?

644. Is there anything you would now do differently on your Human resources management project based on this experience?

645. Are Human resources management project

requirements stable?

646. Have you worked with the customer in the past?

647. Have top software and customer managers formally committed to support the Human resources management project?

648. Maximize short-term return on investment?

649. What should be done with non-critical risks?

650. Are there new risks that mitigation strategies might introduce?

651. Are tool mentors available?

652. Are there risks to human health or the environment that need to be controlled or mitigated?

653. How do you manage Human resources management project Risk?

654. How much risk can you tolerate?

2.32 Risk Register: Human resources management

655. Schedule impact/severity estimated range (workdays) assume the event happens, what is the potential impact?

656. Which key risks have ineffective responses or outstanding improvement actions?

657. What should you do when?

658. Risk probability and impact: how will the probabilities and impacts of risk items be assessed?

659. Have other controls and solutions been implemented in other services which could be applied as an alternative to additional funding?

660. Contingency actions - planned actions to reduce the immediate seriousness of the risk when it does occur. What should you do when?

661. Financial risk -can your organization afford to undertake the Human resources management project?

662. Who is accountable?

663. Market risk -will the new service or product be useful to your organization or marketable to others?

664. How are risks identified?

665. Can the likelihood and impact of failing to achieve corresponding recommendations and action plans be assessed?

666. What is a Risk?

667. Preventative actions - planned actions to reduce the likelihood a risk will occur and/or reduce the seriousness should it occur. What should you do now?

668. What risks might negatively or positively affect achieving the Human resources management project objectives?

669. Having taken action, how did the responses effect change, and where is the Human resources management project now?

670. How well are risks controlled?

671. What would the impact to the Human resources management project objectives be should the risk arise?

672. What has changed since the last period?

673. Cost/benefit – how much will the proposed mitigations cost and how does this cost compare with the potential cost of the risk event/situation should it occur?

2.33 Probability and Impact Assessment: Human resources management

674. Are requirements fully understood by the software engineering team and customers?

675. What is the likely future demand of the customer?

676. Should the risk be taken at all?

677. What can you do about it?

678. What are the industrial relations prevailing in your organization?

679. Do you have specific methods that you use for each phase of the process?

680. What is the risk appetite?

681. Mitigation -how can you avoid the risk?

682. Which role do you have in the Human resources management project?

683. Which of corresponding risk factors can be avoided altogether?

684. Why has this particular mode of contracting been chosen?

685. Is the technology to be built new to your organization?

686. What things might go wrong?

687. Who should be notified of the occurrence of each of the risk indicators?

688. Does the software interface with new or unproven hardware or unproven vendor products?

689. How do the products attain the specifications?

690. Prioritized components/features?

691. Does the Human resources management project team have experience with the technology to be implemented?

692. Do requirements demand the use of new analysis, design, or testing methods?

693. Have you ascribed a level of confidence to every critical technical objective?

2.34 Probability and Impact Matrix: Human resources management

694. Which role do you have in the Human resources management project?

695. How will economic events and trends likely affect the Human resources management project?

696. Workarounds are determined during which risk management process?

697. What would be the effect of slippage?

698. How much is the probability of the risk occurring?

699. During Human resources management project executing, a major problem occurs that was not included in the risk register. What should you do FIRST?

700. Do you train all developers in the process?

701. Are staff committed for the duration of the Human resources management project?

702. Are you on schedule?

703. Are the best people available?

704. How will the consumption pattern change?

705. What are data sources?

706. Have staff received necessary training?

707. What would be the best solution?

708. Are people attending meetings and doing work?

709. How well is the risk understood?

710. Are the risk data timely and relevant?

2.35 Risk Data Sheet: Human resources management

711. How do you handle product safely?

712. How reliable is the data source?

713. What are you weak at and therefore need to do better?

714. What actions can be taken to eliminate or remove risk?

715. What can happen?

716. Whom do you serve (customers)?

717. Will revised controls lead to tolerable risk levels?

718. Has a sensitivity analysis been carried out?

719. What is the environment within which you operate (social trends, economic, community values, broad based participation, national directions etc.)?

720. Are new hazards created?

721. How can hazards be reduced?

722. Has the most cost-effective solution been chosen?

723. How can it happen?

724. What do people affected think about the need for, and practicality of preventive measures?

725. What is the chance that it will happen?

726. Potential for recurrence?

727. Who has a vested interest in how you perform as your organization (our stakeholders)?

728. Risk of what?

729. What can you do?

730. What is the duration of infection (the length of time the host is infected with the organizm) in a normal healthy human host?

2.36 Procurement Management Plan: Human resources management

731. Does the Human resources management project have a Quality Culture?

732. Are Human resources management project team roles and responsibilities identified and documented?

733. Are decisions made in a timely manner?

734. Does the Human resources management project have a Statement of Work?

735. Are changes in scope (deliverable commitments) agreed to by all affected groups & individuals?

736. Is there a Steering Committee in place?

737. Are procurement deliverables arriving on time and to specification?

738. Has a provision been made to reassess Human resources management project risks at various Human resources management project stages?

739. Similar Human resources management projects?

740. Has the schedule been baselined?

741. Are software metrics formally captured, analyzed and used as a basis for other Human resources management project estimates?

742. Human resources management project Objectives?

743. Are Human resources management project team members committed fulltime?

744. Is documentation created for communication with the suppliers and Vendors?

745. Has the Human resources management project manager been identified?

746. Are status reports received per the Human resources management project Plan?

747. Are stakeholders aware and supportive of the principles and practices of modern software estimation?

748. Are Human resources management project leaders committed to this Human resources management project full time?

749. What were things that you did very well and want to do the same again on the next Human resources management project?

750. Does all Human resources management project documentation reside in a common repository for easy access?

2.37 Source Selection Criteria: Human resources management

751. If the costs are normalized, please account for how the normalization is conducted. Is a cost realism analysis used?

752. What should preproposal conferences accomplish?

753. Are evaluators ready to begin this task?

754. Are there any specific considerations that precludes offers from being selected as the awardee?

755. Is experience evaluated?

756. What benefits are accrued from issuing a DRFP in advance of issuing a final RFP?

757. How important is cost in the source selection decision relative to past performance and technical considerations?

758. When is it appropriate to issue a DRFP?

759. How do you consolidate reviews and analysis of evaluators?

760. What common questions or problems are associated with debriefings?

761. Can you reasonably estimate total organization

requirements for the coming year?

762. How can business terms and conditions be improved to yield more effective price competition?

763. How and when do you enter into Human resources management project Procurement Management?

764. Comparison of each offers prices to the estimated prices -are there significant differences?

765. What are the guiding principles for developing an evaluation report?

766. What are the special considerations for preaward debriefings?

767. Do you consider all weaknesses, significant weaknesses, and deficiencies?

768. How much weight should be placed on past performance information?

769. How organization are proposed quotes/prices?

770. What aspects should the contracting officer brief the Human resources management project on prior to evaluation of proposals?

2.38 Stakeholder Management Plan: Human resources management

771. Are trade-offs between accepting the risk and mitigating the risk identified?

772. What has to be purchased?

773. Who will be collecting information?

774. Who is accountable for the achievement of the targeted outcome(s) and reports on the progress towards the target?

775. What is meant by activity dependencies and how do they relate to network diagramming?

776. Is stakeholder involvement adequate?

777. Were Human resources management project team members involved in detailed estimating and scheduling?

778. What are reporting requirements?

779. Are there checklists created to demine if all quality processes are followed?

780. How are the overall Human resources management project development processes to be undertaken to produce the Human resources management project outputs?

781. Is the assigned Human resources management project manager a PMP (Certified Human resources management project manager) and experienced?

782. Who will be responsible for managing and maintaining the Issues Register?

2.39 Change Management Plan: Human resources management

783. Have the systems been configured and tested?

784. How prevalent is Resistance to Change?

785. What is the most positive interpretation it can receive?

786. Has an information & communications plan been developed?

787. What are the needs, priorities and special interests of the audience?

788. Has the priority for this Human resources management project been set by the Business Unit Management Team?

789. Clearly articulate the overall business benefits of the Human resources management project -why are you doing this now?

790. Do there need to be new channels developed?

791. What goal(s) do you hope to accomplish?

792. Have the approved procedures and policies been published?

793. What are the key change management success metrics?

794. What are the specific target groups / audience that will be impacted by this change?

795. What is the most cynical response it can receive?

796. Who will be the change levers?

797. Has the target training audience been identified and nominated?

798. What are the current methods of sharing information and do there need to be new ones developed?

799. Do you need new systems?

800. What is the reason for the communication?

801. What are the essentials of the message?

802. Who is the target audience of the piece of information?

3.0 Executing Process Group: Human resources management

803. What are the main types of contracts if you do decide to outsource?

804. What communication items need improvement?

805. Is the Human resources management project making progress in helping to achieve the set results?

806. How does the job market and current state of the economy affect human resource management?

807. What areas does the group agree are the biggest success on the Human resources management project?

808. How do you enter durations, link tasks, and view critical path information?

809. If action is called for, what form should it take?

810. Measurable - are the targets measurable?

811. Do the products created live up to the necessary quality?

812. Does software appear easy to learn?

813. What are the main types of goods and services being outsourced?

814. If a risk event occurs, what will you do?

815. When do you share the scorecard with managers?

816. What are the main parts of the scope statement?

817. How well defined and documented were the Human resources management project management processes you chose to use?

818. After how many days will the lease cost be the same as the purchase cost for the equipment?

3.1 Team Member Status Report: Human resources management

819. The problem with Reward & Recognition Programs is that the truly deserving people all too often get left out. How can you make it practical?

820. Are the attitudes of staff regarding Human resources management project work improving?

821. Why is it to be done?

822. How does this product, good, or service meet the needs of the Human resources management project and your organization as a whole?

823. How much risk is involved?

824. When a teams productivity and success depend on collaboration and the efficient flow of information, what generally fails them?

825. Are your organizations Human resources management projects more successful over time?

826. Is there evidence that staff is taking a more professional approach toward management of your organizations Human resources management projects?

827. Will the staff do training or is that done by a third party?

828. What is to be done?

829. Does your organization have the means (staff, money, contract, etc.) to produce or to acquire the product, good, or service?

830. How will resource planning be done?

831. What specific interest groups do you have in place?

832. Are the products of your organizations Human resources management projects meeting customers objectives?

833. Does the product, good, or service already exist within your organization?

834. Do you have an Enterprise Human resources management project Management Office (EPMO)?

835. How can you make it practical?

836. How it is to be done?

837. Does every department have to have a Human resources management project Manager on staff?

3.2 Change Request: Human resources management

838. Who is communicating the change?

839. Are there requirements attributes that are strongly related to the complexity and size?

840. Has a formal technical review been conducted to assess technical correctness?

841. Why do you want to have a change control system?

842. What mechanism is used to appraise others of changes that are made?

843. What are the requirements for urgent changes?

844. What is the relationship between requirements attributes and attributes like complexity and size?

845. How can you ensure that changes have been made properly?

846. How does a team identify the discrete elements of a configuration?

847. How do team members communicate with each other?

848. For which areas does this operating procedure apply?

849. How are changes requested (forms, method of communication)?

850. Screen shots or attachments included in a Change Request?

851. How many lines of code must be changed to implement the change?

852. Which requirements attributes affect the risk to reliability the most?

853. How are changes graded and who is responsible for the rating?

854. Will all change requests be unconditionally tracked through this process?

855. What type of changes does change control take into account?

856. Has the change been highlighted and documented in the CSCI?

3.3 Change Log: Human resources management

857. When was the request submitted?

858. Do the described changes impact on the integrity or security of the system?

859. Is the change request within Human resources management project scope?

860. Is the change request open, closed or pending?

861. Who initiated the change request?

862. Does the suggested change request represent a desired enhancement to the products functionality?

863. Is the requested change request a result of changes in other Human resources management project(s)?

864. Is the submitted change a new change or a modification of a previously approved change?

865. How does this change affect the timeline of the schedule?

866. Is the change backward compatible without limitations?

867. Should a more thorough impact analysis be conducted?

868. Is this a mandatory replacement?

869. How does this relate to the standards developed for specific business processes?

870. Will the Human resources management project fail if the change request is not executed?

871. How does this change affect scope?

872. When was the request approved?

873. Where do changes come from?

874. Does the suggested change request seem to represent a necessary enhancement to the product?

3.4 Decision Log: Human resources management

875. Behaviors; what are guidelines that the team has identified that will assist them with getting the most out of team meetings?

876. What alternatives/risks were considered?

877. How do you know when you are achieving it?

878. Meeting purpose; why does this team meet?

879. With whom was the decision shared or considered?

880. What are the cost implications?

881. Which variables make a critical difference?

882. Does anything need to be adjusted?

883. Decision-making process; how will the team make decisions?

884. How does an increasing emphasis on cost containment influence the strategies and tactics used?

885. What makes you different or better than others companies selling the same thing?

886. At what point in time does loss become

unacceptable?

887. Is everything working as expected?

888. Adversarial environment. is your opponent open to a non-traditional workflow, or will it likely challenge anything you do?

889. What is your overall strategy for quality control / quality assurance procedures?

890. How does provision of information, both in terms of content and presentation, influence acceptance of alternative strategies?

891. What eDiscovery problem or issue did your organization set out to fix or make better?

892. How effective is maintaining the log at facilitating organizational learning?

893. How does the use a Decision Support System influence the strategies/tactics or costs?

894. How consolidated and comprehensive a story can you tell by capturing currently available incident data in a central location and through a log of key decisions during an incident?

3.5 Quality Audit: Human resources management

895. How does the organization know that its system for maintaining and advancing the capabilities of its staff, particularly in relation to the Mission of the organization, is appropriately effective and constructive?

896. Are all areas associated with the storage and reconditioning of devices clean, free of rubbish, adequately ventilated and in good repair?

897. Does the audit organization have experience in performing the required work for entities of your type and size?

898. How does your organization know that it is maintaining a conducive staff climate?

899. How does your organization know that its management system is appropriately effective and constructive?

900. How does your organization know that its staff are presenting original work, and properly acknowledging the work of others?

901. How does your organization know that its staff support services planning and management systems are appropriately effective and constructive?

902. How does your organization know that the

support for its staff is appropriately effective and constructive?

903. Do all staff have the necessary authority and resources to deliver what is expected of them?

904. How does your organization know that its planning processes are appropriately effective and constructive?

905. How does your organization know that its staff financial services are appropriately effective and constructive?

906. Are all complaints involving the possible failure of a device, labeling, or packaging to meet any of its specifications reviewed, evaluated, and investigated?

907. How does your organization know that its Strategic Plan is providing the best guidance for the future of your organization?

908. Are training programs documented?

909. How does your organization know that its system for recruiting the best staff possible are appropriately effective and constructive?

910. How does your organization know that its system for inducting new staff to maximize workplace contributions are appropriately effective and constructive?

911. How are you auditing your organizations compliance with regulations?

912. How does your organization know that its systems for assisting staff with career planning and employment placements are appropriately effective and constructive?

913. Is there any content that may be legally actionable?

3.6 Team Directory: Human resources management

914. Who are your stakeholders (customers, sponsors, end users, team members)?

915. Who will write the meeting minutes and distribute?

916. What are you going to deliver or accomplish?

917. Who are the Team Members?

918. Where will the product be used and/or delivered or built when appropriate?

919. What needs to be communicated?

920. How and in what format should information be presented?

921. Process decisions: are all start-up, turn over and close out requirements of the contract satisfied?

922. How will the team handle changes?

923. Who will talk to the customer?

924. When will you produce deliverables?

925. Process decisions: which organizational elements and which individuals will be assigned management functions?

926. Do purchase specifications and configurations match requirements?

927. Timing: when do the effects of communication take place?

928. Process decisions: are there any statutory or regulatory issues relevant to the timely execution of work?

929. Decisions: is the most suitable form of contract being used?

930. Is construction on schedule?

931. How does the team resolve conflicts and ensure tasks are completed?

3.7 Team Operating Agreement: Human resources management

932. Methodologies: how will key team processes be implemented, such as training, research, work deliverable production, review and approval processes, knowledge management, and meeting procedures?

933. Do you use a parking lot for any items that are important and outside of the agenda?

934. Did you prepare participants for the next meeting?

935. Do you brief absent members after they view meeting notes or listen to a recording?

936. Has the appropriate access to relevant data and analysis capability been granted?

937. How will group handle unplanned absences?

938. What is culture?

939. What are the current caseload numbers in the unit?

940. What individual strengths does each team member bring to the group?

941. Conflict resolution: how will disputes and other conflicts be mediated or resolved?

942. Do you leverage technology engagement tools group chat, polls, screen sharing, etc.?

943. The method to be used in the decision making process; Will it be consensus, majority rule, or the supervisor having the final say?

944. Resource allocation: how will individual team members account for time and expenses, and how will this be allocated in the team budget?

945. Do you prevent individuals from dominating the meeting?

946. Did you determine the technology methods that best match the messages to be communicated?

947. Do you record meetings for the already stated unable to attend?

948. Communication protocols: how will the team communicate?

949. Are there more than two national cultures represented by your team?

950. Confidentiality: how will confidential information be handled?

951. Are there influences outside the team that may affect performance, and if so, have you identified and addressed them?

3.8 Team Performance Assessment: Human resources management

952. Where to from here?

953. Do friends perform better than acquaintances?

954. Lack of method variance in self-reported affect and perceptions at work: Reality or artifact?

955. To what degree does the teams purpose contain themes that are particularly meaningful and memorable?

956. To what degree does the teams purpose constitute a broader, deeper aspiration than just accomplishing short-term goals?

957. To what degree can team members meet frequently enough to accomplish the teams ends?

958. To what degree will the team ensure that all members equitably share the work essential to the success of the team?

959. Is there a particular method of data analysis that you would recommend as a means of demonstrating that method variance is not of great concern for a given dataset?

960. To what degree does the teams work approach provide opportunity for members to engage in fact-based problem solving?

961. To what degree do all members feel responsible for all agreed-upon measures?

962. How hard do you try to make a good selection?

963. To what degree does the teams approach to its work allow for modification and improvement over time?

964. To what degree will the team adopt a concrete, clearly understood, and agreed-upon approach that will result in achievement of the teams goals?

965. How do you encourage members to learn from each other?

966. To what degree is there a sense that only the team can succeed?

967. To what degree can team members frequently and easily communicate with one another?

968. How much interpersonal friction is there in your team?

969. When does the medium matter?

970. What makes opportunities more or less obvious?

971. To what degree will the approach capitalize on and enhance the skills of all team members in a manner that takes into consideration other demands on members of the team?

3.9 Team Member Performance Assessment: Human resources management

972. How are evaluation results utilized?

973. What are the standards or expectations for success?

974. Which training platform formats (i.e., mobile, virtual, videogame-based) were implemented in your effort(s)?

975. Are any validation activities performed?

976. What happens if a team member receives a Rating of Unsatisfactory?

977. What are they responsible for?

978. Does the rater (supervisor) have to wait for the interim or final performance assessment review to tell an employee that the employees performance is unsatisfactory?

979. To what degree do team members articulate the teams work approach?

980. To what degree do team members understand one anothers roles and skills?

981. How is performance assessment used in making future award decisions including options and extend/

compete decisions?

982. Should a ratee get a copy of all the raters documents about the employees performance?

983. Are assessment validation activities performed?

984. To what degree does the team possess adequate membership to achieve its ends?

985. To what degree are sub-teams possible or necessary?

986. What is collaboration?

987. What are best practices for delivering and developing training evaluations to maximize the benefits of leveraging emerging technologies?

988. To what degree will new and supplemental skills be introduced as the need is recognized?

989. Why were corresponding selected?

990. What changes do you need to make to align practices with beliefs?

3.10 Issue Log: Human resources management

991. What is the stakeholders political influence?

992. What effort will a change need?

993. Who is the issue assigned to?

994. How were past initiatives successful?

995. Who were proponents/opponents?

996. Is access to the Issue Log controlled?

997. Why not more evaluators?

998. What does the stakeholder need from the team?

999. Who needs to know and how much?

1000. Do you prepare stakeholder engagement plans?

1001. What approaches to you feel are the best ones to use?

1002. What is the status of the issue?

1003. How do you manage human resources?

1004. How do you reply to this question; you am new here and managing this major program. How do you suggest you build your network?

1005. Why do you manage human resources?

1006. How do you manage communications?

1007. Why multiple evaluators?

4.0 Monitoring and Controlling Process Group: Human resources management

1008. How should needs be met?

1009. What do they need to know about the Human resources management project?

1010. Just how important is your work to the overall success of the Human resources management project?

1011. What are the deliverables?

1012. What areas were overlooked on this Human resources management project?

1013. User: who wants the information and what are they interested in?

1014. When will the Human resources management project be done?

1015. How well did the chosen processes produce the expected results?

1016. What resources (both financial and non-financial) are available/needed?

1017. What were things that you did very well and want to do the same again on the next Human resources management project?

1018. How is agile program management done?

1019. Is the program in place as intended?

1020. Were escalated issues resolved promptly?

1021. How well did you do?

1022. Change, where should you look for problems?

1023. Is the program making progress in helping to achieve the set results?

1024. How to ensure validity, quality and consistency?

4.1 Project Performance Report: Human resources management

1025. To what degree does the informal organization make use of individual resources and meet individual needs?

1026. To what degree are the demands of the task compatible with and converge with the relationships of the informal organization?

1027. To what degree do team members frequently explore the teams purpose and its implications?

1028. To what degree does the task meet individual needs?

1029. To what degree does the information network provide individuals with the information they require?

1030. To what degree do the goals specify concrete team work products?

1031. To what degree do individual skills and abilities match task demands?

1032. To what degree are fresh input and perspectives systematically caught and added (for example, through information and analysis, new members, and senior sponsors)?

1033. To what degree are the goals realistic?

1034. How will procurement be coordinated with other Human resources management project aspects, such as scheduling and performance reporting?

1035. What is the PRS?

1036. To what degree does the funding match the requirement?

1037. To what degree do the structures of the formal organization motivate taskrelevant behavior and facilitate task completion?

1038. To what degree does the teams work approach provide opportunity for members to engage in open interaction?

1039. To what degree does the teams work approach provide opportunity for members to engage in results-based evaluation?

4.2 Variance Analysis: Human resources management

1040. What costs are avoidable if one or more customers are dropped?

1041. Do work packages consist of discrete tasks which are adequately described?

1042. Do you identify potential or actual budget-based and time-based schedule variances?

1043. What is your organizations rationale for sharing expenses and services between business segments?

1044. What is the expected future profitability of each customer?

1045. Is data disseminated to the contractors management timely, accurate, and usable?

1046. How do you identify and isolate causes of favorable and unfavorable cost and schedule variances?

1047. Are management actions taken to reduce indirect costs when there are significant adverse variances?

1048. How does the use of a single conversion element (rather than the traditional labor and overhead elements) affect standard costing?

1049. Historical experience?

1050. What does a favorable labor efficiency variance mean?

1051. Are control accounts opened and closed based on the start and completion of work contained therein?

1052. Did a new competitor enter the market?

1053. Is there a logical explanation for any variance?

1054. Are the actual costs used for variance analysis reconcilable with data from the accounting system?

1055. How are material, labor, and overhead standards set?

1056. Are the wbs and organizational levels for application of the Human resources management projected overhead costs identified?

1057. Wbs elements contractually specified for reporting of status to your organization (lowest level only)?

4.3 Earned Value Status: Human resources management

1058. Earned value can be used in almost any Human resources management project situation and in almost any Human resources management project environment. it may be used on large Human resources management projects, medium sized Human resources management projects, tiny Human resources management projects (in cut-down form), complex and simple Human resources management projects and in any market sector. some people, of course, know all about earned value, they have used it for years - but perhaps not as effectively as they could have?

1059. Verification is a process of ensuring that the developed system satisfies the stakeholders agreements and specifications; Are you building the product right? What do you verify?

1060. Where is evidence-based earned value in your organization reported?

1061. When is it going to finish?

1062. Where are your problem areas?

1063. Validation is a process of ensuring that the developed system will actually achieve the stakeholders desired outcomes; Are you building the right product? What do you validate?

1064. If earned value management (EVM) is so good in determining the true status of a Human resources management project and Human resources management project its completion, why is it that hardly any one uses it in information systems related Human resources management projects?

1065. How does this compare with other Human resources management projects?

1066. What is the unit of forecast value?

1067. Are you hitting your Human resources management projects targets?

1068. How much is it going to cost by the finish?

4.4 Risk Audit: Human resources management

1069. Do you have a clear plan for the future that describes what you want to do and how you are going to do it?

1070. What is the effect of globalisation; is business becoming too complex and can the auditor rely on auditing standards?

1071. Do you have written and signed agreements/contracts in place for each paid staff member?

1072. Do you promote education and training opportunities?

1073. Who audits the auditor?

1074. Improving fraud detection: do auditors react to abnormal inconsistencies between financial and non-financial measures?

1075. Are there any forms the staff is required to sign?

1076. Are all participants informed of safety issues?

1077. Does your organization have any policies or procedures to guide its decision-making (code of conduct for the board, conflict of interest policy, etc.)?

1078. What are the differences and similarities between strategic and operational risks in your organization?

1079. Does your auditor understand your business?

1080. Is your organization willing to commit significant time to the requirements gathering process?

1081. Do you record and file all audits?

1082. Is your organization an exempt employer for payroll tax purposes?

1083. What can be measured?

1084. To what extent are auditors effective at linking business risks and management assertions?

1085. What are risks and how do you manage them?

1086. Does your organization communicate regularly and effectively with its members?

1087. How effective are your risk controls?

4.5 Contractor Status Report: Human resources management

1088. If applicable; describe your standard schedule for new software version releases. Are new software version releases included in the standard maintenance plan?

1089. What was the budget or estimated cost for your organizations services?

1090. How is risk transferred?

1091. How long have you been using the services?

1092. What was the actual budget or estimated cost for your organizations services?

1093. What process manages the contracts?

1094. Are there contractual transfer concerns?

1095. How does the proposed individual meet each requirement?

1096. What was the overall budget or estimated cost?

1097. What was the final actual cost?

1098. Who can list a Human resources management project as organization experience, your organization or a previous employee of your organization?

1099. What is the average response time for answering a support call?

1100. Describe how often regular updates are made to the proposed solution. Are corresponding regular updates included in the standard maintenance plan?

1101. What are the minimum and optimal bandwidth requirements for the proposed soluiton?

4.6 Formal Acceptance: Human resources management

1102. What lessons were learned about your Human resources management project management methodology?

1103. General estimate of the costs and times to complete the Human resources management project?

1104. Did the Human resources management project manager and team act in a professional and ethical manner?

1105. Was the sponsor/customer satisfied?

1106. Do you perform formal acceptance or burn-in tests?

1107. What function(s) does it fill or meet?

1108. How does your team plan to obtain formal acceptance on your Human resources management project?

1109. Was business value realized?

1110. Did the Human resources management project achieve its MOV?

1111. What are the requirements against which to test, Who will execute?

1112. What is the Acceptance Management Process?

1113. What features, practices, and processes proved to be strengths or weaknesses?

1114. Was the Human resources management project goal achieved?

1115. What can you do better next time?

1116. Have all comments been addressed?

1117. Was the client satisfied with the Human resources management project results?

1118. Does it do what Human resources management project team said it would?

1119. Who supplies data?

1120. Was the Human resources management project work done on time, within budget, and according to specification?

1121. Who would use it?

5.0 Closing Process Group: Human resources management

1122. Did the Human resources management project team have enough people to execute the Human resources management project plan?

1123. How well defined and documented were the Human resources management project management processes you chose to use?

1124. How will you know you did it?

1125. What is the risk of failure to your organization?

1126. What can you do better next time, and what specific actions can you take to improve?

1127. Did the Human resources management project management methodology work?

1128. When will the Human resources management project be done?

1129. What were the desired outcomes?

1130. What areas does the group agree are the biggest success on the Human resources management project?

1131. What could be done to improve the process?

1132. What business situation is being addressed?

1133. How dependent is the Human resources management project on other Human resources management projects or work efforts?

1134. What areas were overlooked on this Human resources management project?

1135. Does the close educate others to improve performance?

1136. What were things that you did very well and want to do the same again on the next Human resources management project?

5.1 Procurement Audit: Human resources management

1137. Do the internal control systems function appropriate?

1138. Does the cash disbursement policy prohibit drawing checks to cash or bearer?

1139. Who are the key suppliers?

1140. Does the strategy ensure that needs are met, and not exceeded?

1141. Are all purchase orders cancelled after payment to avoid duplicate payment of the same invoice?

1142. Does the approval include approval of prices?

1143. If information was withheld, was there reasonable justification for this decision?

1144. Is there an overall mission for the procurement function/unit and is it determined which tasks the procurement function/unit should carry out?

1145. Is a physical inventory taken periodically to verify fixed asset records?

1146. Are review meetings organized during contract execution and do they meet demand?

1147. Are proper authorization and approval required

prior to payment?

1148. How do you deal with budget constrains and assurance needs?

1149. Were additional works brought about by a cause which had not previously existed?

1150. Does the procurement function/unit have the ability to apply electronic procurement?

1151. Are advantages and disadvantages of in-house production, outsourcing and Public Private Partnerships considered?

1152. Was all the key documentation given to the contracting authority?

1153. Are procurement policies and practices in line with (international) good practice standards?

1154. Is the functioning of automatic disbursement programs tested by an independent party?

1155. Are the purchase order forms designed for efficient and simple completion?

1156. Are the journals and ledgers kept current for all funds?

5.2 Contract Close-Out: Human resources management

1157. What happens to the recipient of services?

1158. Change in circumstances?

1159. How does it work?

1160. Was the contract complete without requiring numerous changes and revisions?

1161. How is the contracting office notified of the automatic contract close-out?

1162. Parties: Authorized?

1163. Have all contracts been completed?

1164. Was the contract type appropriate?

1165. Change in knowledge?

1166. What is capture management?

1167. Have all contract records been included in the Human resources management project archives?

1168. Have all acceptance criteria been met prior to final payment to contractors?

1169. How/when used ?

1170. Parties: who is involved?

1171. Was the contract sufficiently clear so as not to result in numerous disputes and misunderstandings?

1172. Are the signers the authorized officials?

1173. Have all contracts been closed?

1174. Change in attitude or behavior?

1175. Has each contract been audited to verify acceptance and delivery?

1176. Why Outsource?

5.3 Project or Phase Close-Out: Human resources management

1177. What hierarchical authority does the stakeholder have in your organization?

1178. What was expected from each stakeholder?

1179. Did the Human resources management project management methodology work?

1180. What stakeholder group needs, expectations, and interests are being met by the Human resources management project?

1181. What is this stakeholder expecting?

1182. If you were the Human resources management project sponsor, how would you determine which Human resources management project team(s) and/ or individuals deserve recognition?

1183. When and how were information needs best met?

1184. What went well?

1185. Have business partners been involved extensively, and what data was required for them?

1186. Was the schedule met?

1187. Was the user/client satisfied with the end

product?

1188. What process was planned for managing issues/risks?

1189. In addition to assessing whether the Human resources management project was successful, it is equally critical to analyze why it was or was not fully successful. Are you including this?

1190. Who controlled the resources for the Human resources management project?

1191. Is the lesson significant, valid, and applicable?

1192. What security considerations needed to be addressed during the procurement life cycle?

1193. What was learned?

1194. What are the marketing communication needs for each stakeholder?

5.4 Lessons Learned: Human resources management

1195. What things mattered the most on this Human resources management project?

1196. How well did the scope of the Human resources management project match what was defined in the Human resources management project Proposal?

1197. What things surprised you on the Human resources management project that were not in the plan?

1198. Under what legal authority did your organization head and program manager direct your organization and Human resources management project?

1199. How clearly defined were the objectives for this Human resources management project?

1200. How well prepared were you to receive Human resources management project deliverables?

1201. Did the delivered product meet the specified requirements and goals of the Human resources management project?

1202. Who managed most of the communication within the Human resources management project?

1203. How effective was the documentation that you

received with the Human resources management project product/service?

1204. How effective was the training you received in preparation for the use of the product/service?

1205. How closely did deliverables match what was defined within the Human resources management project Scope?

1206. How effective was Human resources management project Team member training?

1207. Does the lesson describe a function that would be done differently the next time?

1208. What Human resources management project circumstances were not anticipated?

1209. What regulatory regime controlled how your organization head and program manager directed your organization and Human resources management project?

1210. How effective were the techniques used to prepare you and your organization for the impact of the changes brought about by the product or service produced by the Human resources management project?

1211. How actively and meaningfully were stakeholders involved in the Human resources management project?

1212. How well does the product or service the Human resources management project produced meet your needs?

1213. Is your organization willing to expose problems or mistakes for the betterment of the collective whole, and can you do this in a way that does not intimidate employees or workers?

Index

250

producing   129
product   1, 12, 42, 53-54, 84, 86, 89, 125, 167-168, 171, 185, 191, 203-204, 208, 214, 230, 245-247
production   62, 216, 241
productive   175
products   1, 18, 21, 45, 101, 117, 129, 156, 171, 188, 201, 204, 207, 226
profit   172
profits   167
program   23, 60, 118, 120, 178, 222, 225, 246-247
programme   117
programs   121, 155, 182, 203, 212, 241
progress   30, 38, 64, 84, 87, 93, 106, 115, 141, 161, 166, 174, 197, 201, 225
prohibit   240
project 2-4, 6-8, 10, 19, 21-22, 24, 34, 42, 54, 72, 75, 82, 90, 93-94, 96-97, 100, 103, 106, 109-118, 120-126, 130-132, 135-137, 141-150, 153-155, 157-170, 175, 177-181, 183-189, 193-194, 196-199, 201-204, 207-208, 224, 226-227, 230-231, 234, 236-239, 242, 244-247
projected   167, 175-176, 229
projects   2, 85, 94, 109, 117, 121, 129, 135, 137, 159, 178, 182, 193, 203-204, 230-231, 239
promising   86
promote   29, 45, 52, 232
promotion   177
promptly   225
proofing   64
proper 240
properly   12, 26-27, 46, 110, 128, 176, 205, 211
proponents   222
proposal   147-148, 246
proposals   79, 196
proposed   21, 39, 60, 64, 115, 120-121, 186, 196, 234-235
protect   53, 97
protection   91
protocols   217
proved 237
provide   23, 51, 83, 87, 95, 114, 128, 140, 158, 165, 171, 175, 218, 226-227
provided   9, 14, 79, 124, 135
providing   112, 114, 132, 147, 212
provision   193, 210

CPSIA information can be obtained
at www.ICGtesting.com
Printed in the USA
BVHW080841220419
546159BV00026B/1758/P